Table of Contents

Practice Test #1

Practice Questions

1. A family wherein the parents, children, and grandmother live together is defined as a(n):
   a. Nuclear family
   b. Extended family
   c. Blended family
   d. Combined family

2. Research finds that a large proportion of adults working in demanding fields like politics and medicine most often had which birth order in their families?
   a. Middle children
   b. Second children
   c. Youngest children
   d. First-born children

3. Compared to families of the past, today's families are more often geographically isolated from their relatives at which socioeconomic level?
   a. Lower-middle-class families
   b. Upper-middle-class families
   c. Middle-class families
   d. Lower-class families

4. Which of the following is currently accurate legally regarding blended families?
   a. Children may not accept their parenting, but stepparents legally become their parents.
   b. Stepparents are not legally recognized as parents unless they adopt the spouse's child.
   c. If a parent and stepparent get divorced, laws give visitation rights to the ex-stepparent.
   d. The law is unclear regarding stepparents, so rights are decided on a case-by-case basis.

5. When a parent is widowed or divorced, toddlers may react more to:
   a. Options (B) and (C) both rather than option (D) only.
   b. Changes in familiar routines than the loss of a parent.
   c. How that parent copes than loss of the other parent.
   d. Parent loss than parental coping or changed routines.

6. In which stage of family development do activities shared by spouses typically decrease dramatically?
   a. The expanding years
   b. The developing years
   c. The launching years
   d. The middle years

7. According to some models of family life stages, which stage includes a developmental task of establishing the foundations for a model of family life?
    a. The stage that involves leaving the home
    b. The stage of family of origin experiences
    c. The stage of becoming a childless couple
    d. The stage just prior to becoming married

8. Which of the following best reflects a disadvantage of stage theories regarding families?
    a. The stages express typical family concerns in each stage.
    b. Stage theories provide convenient common vocabularies.
    c. They focus on dynamics the same as systems theories do.
    d. Many diverse families today are not normative or typical.

9. In Piaget's theory of cognitive development, the thinking of children in the later part of the Preoperational stage becomes less egocentric, but still remains animistic and magical. This corresponds to which tasks in Duvall's family development theory?
    a. Encouraging the child to fit into the community and to participate in education
    b. Helping the child find a balance of freedom and responsibility; career interests
    c. Adapting to the child's needs; coping with lack of privacy and depleted energy
    d. Stages of establishment, expectancy, and integration of a child into the family

10. In his attachment theory regarding parents and children, John Bowlby defined four elements of attachment. Which of these did he say enables a young child to explore the environment?
    a. A secure base
    b. The safe haven
    c. Separation distress
    d. Proximity maintenance

11. In her work identifying parenting styles, Diana Baumrind defined four dimensions of interactions between parents and children. Which of these dimensions is most related to parental tendencies to reason with their children to elicit the behaviors they want?
    a. Nurturance
    b. Parental control
    c. Clarity of communication
    d. Maturity demands

12. Baumrind and other researchers applying her theory of parenting styles have found that children reared by parents with the authoritarian style are most likely to become:
    a. Independent, responsible high achievers
    b. Immature, irresponsible, impulse-ridden
    c. Obedient, anxious, and moody followers
    d. Depressed, low-functioning delinquents

13. Schaefer (1959) conceptualized parenting styles along continua across two dimensions:
    a. Love vs. control and autonomy vs. hostility
    b. Neglect-punishment, dependence-demand
    c. Love vs. hostility and autonomy vs. control
    d. Strict vs. accepting and permissive vs. rejecting

14. Which of the following most accurately represents a concept of Bandura's social learning theory?
    a. Children can learn vicariously by observing and imitating others' behaviors.
    b. Children only learn directly through consequences of their own behaviors.
    c. Children observe and imitate others' behaviors but do not learn from this.
    d. Children learn better from positive reinforcement than from punishment.

15. Which of these did Albert Bandura discover in studying the influence of media on children?
    a. Young children's behavior is unaffected because they cannot tell reality from fantasy.
    b. Children imitate violent behaviors, but not altruistic behaviors when they view these.
    c. Children who viewed violent video material displayed increased aggressive behaviors.
    d. Children who viewed violent video material displayed fearfulness but not aggression.

16. Among the things parents provide for their children, which would be at the bottom of the pyramid in Maslow's hierarchy of needs?
    a. Giving love, ensuring they feel they belong
    b. Ensuring they get adequate food and sleep
    c. Making sure they have shelter and security
    d. Building self-esteem and feelings of worth

17. Things like the way family members communicate with one another, family members' eating habits, and what kinds of friends the different family members have are most related to:
    a. Structure of a family
    b. Resources of a family
    c. The roles in a family
    d. Lifestyles of a family

18. Many researchers have found that family recreation affords benefits both to the family unit and to its individual members. Of the following, which reflects a benefit to individual family members?
    a. Improvements in communication
    b. The development of lifelong skills
    c. Increased stability and interaction
    d. The maintenance of relationships

19. In which of Erikson's stages does a child first develop awareness of different social roles in the environment?
    a. Trust vs. Mistrust
    b. Industry vs. Inferiority
    c. Initiative vs. Guilt
    d. Identity vs. Confusion

20. According to Gesell's stages of development, at which of the following ages are children most cooperative with their parents?
    a. 8 years
    b. 6 years
    c. 10 years
    d. 9 years

21. According to Robert Havighurst, in which stage do an individual's developmental tasks include learning to relate the self emotionally to other members of the family?
    a. Middle Childhood (6 to 12 years)
    b. Pre-Adolescence, Adolescence (12 to 18 years)
    c. Infancy and Early Childhood (0 to 6 years)
    d. Early Adulthood (18 to 35 years)

22. Piaget viewed child development in social and moral contexts as a progression from
    a. Anomy to heteronomy to autonomy.
    b. Heteronomy to autonomy to anomy.
    c. Autonomy to anomy to heteronomy.
    d. Heteronomy to anomy to autonomy.

23. To a newborn infant, which of Maslow's levels of needs is most important?
    a. Love, belonging
    b. Safety, security
    c. Self-actualizing
    d. Physiological

24. Cognitively developing understanding of basic cause-and-effect and object categorization are developmental tasks in which life stage?
    a. 2 to 4 years
    b. 4 to 6 years
    c. Birth to 2 years
    d. 6 to 12 years

25. Which of the following is NOT a typical developmental task for children at the earliest school ages?
    a. Conservation of amount
    b. Identifying with sex roles
    c. Developing early morality
    d. Learning to play in groups

26. In which life stage is it most common for adults to redirect their energy to new activities and roles?
    a. The middle adult ages
    b. During later adulthood
    c. During early adulthood
    d. In adulthood's old age

27. An individual with the developmental disability of cerebral palsy is *most* likely to need special responses and resources addressing which area?
    a. Motor development
    b. Cognitive development
    c. Emotional development
    d. Social skills development

28. Learning in the same way as others but at an overall slower rate is *most* descriptive of which developmental disability?
    a. The autism spectrum
    b. Intellectual disability
    c. Sensory impairment
    d. A learning disability

29. According to Urie Bronfenbrenner's ecological systems theory of development, in which system does an individual experience the most interpersonal and social interactions?
    a. The exosystem
    b. The mesosystem
    c. The macrosystem
    d. The microsystem

30. According to Freud, in early childhood a boy must do which of these to enable him thereafter to have healthy interpersonal relationships?
    a. Not have an Oedipal conflict
    b. Resolve the Oedipal conflict
    c. Maintain an Oedipal conflict
    d. Experience Oedipal conflict

31. According to Murray Bowen's Family Systems Theory, which type of person has poor differentiation of self, depends on acceptance and approval, and is threatened by disagreement?
    a. "Chameleons" who conform to please others
    b. Bullies who pressure others to conform/agree
    c. This describes neither chameleons nor bullies.
    d. Both chameleons and bullies fit the description.

32. Among family roles identified by Virginia Satir, which of these is considered healthy and effective?
    a. Blaming others
    b. None of these
    c. Pleasing others
    d. Diverting others

33. Regarding communication patterns, which of the following is accurate?
    a. High-context communication uses a clear, firmer voice.
    b. Low-context communication uses the nonverbal more.
    c. Low-context communication has an indirect verbal style.
    d. High-context communication is indirect communication.

34. What do interpreter-sensitive values mean relative to communication styles?
    a. The listener is expected to be responsible for interpreting meaning.
    b. The speaker is expected to be responsible for giving a clear message.
    c. The speaker avoids nonverbal behaviors for the listener to interpret.
    d. The listener need not "read between the lines" as decoding is simple.

35. Which of the following is accurate about what is communicated nonverbally by the gesture we call "thumbs up" in the USA?
    a. This gesture has a globally universal meaning only when hitchhiking.
    b. This gesture has completely different meanings in various countries.
    c. This gesture has a different meaning but only one meaning in Japan.
    d. This gesture has multiple meanings in some nations but not America.

36. For conflict prevention, which of these is an example of cooperative communication rather than of person-centered expressions that put others on the defensive?
    a. "You always interrupt me before I can finish what I'm saying."
    b. "It will help me to finish, and then I want to hear your ideas."
    c. "Can't you just be quiet and listen to me for even a minute?"
    d. "You don't know what you're talking about. You don't listen."

37. What is correct regarding Freud's and Erikson's theories of development relative to the life span?
    a. Freud's theory does not cover the entire life span, but Erikson's does.
    b. Erikson's theory does not cover the entire life span, but Freud's does.
    c. Neither Freud nor Erikson covered the entire life span in either theory.
    d. Both Freud's and Erikson's theories do encompass the entire life span.

38. Which consumer rights and responsibilities are addressed by the establishment of the Office of Fair Lending and Equal Opportunity under the Wall Street Reform and Consumer Protection Act of 2009?
    a. (B) and (D)
    b. To redress
    c. To be heard
    d. To choice

39. Which of the following is an example of a consumer responsibility?
    a. To make one's concerns heard to those who can address the concerns
    b. To have one's voice heard about product development and lawmaking
    c. To be able to choose among an abundant variety of goods and services
    d. To access information that assures the veracity of product statements

40. Which of the following includes the consumer's right to a healthy environment?
    a. The Consumer Product Safety Commission
    b. The UN Consumer Protection Guidelines
    c. The Underwriters' Laboratories
    d. The Bureau of Competition

41. Research finds consumers are less interested in using price data to inform their health care decisions under which of these conditions?
    a. The consumers incur high out-of-pocket expenses
    b. The consumers like the doctor that they are seeing
    c. The consumers' medical conditions are nonurgent
    d. The consumers have few provider preconceptions

42. In making good consumer decisions, which of the following should smart shoppers do first?
    a. Narrow the field of potential choices
    b. List attributes of products or services
    c. Determine their needs as consumers
    d. The order of doing these is irrelevant.

43. For financial planning, which of the following should an individual or family do first?
    a. Developing what their financial goals will be
    b. Identifying alternative actions they will take
    c. Evaluating consequences of various actions
    d. Determining their current financial situation

44. We are advised to analyze our financial goals and values periodically to aid in financial planning. What is true about this process?
    a. The reason for analysis is to distinguish between wants and needs.
    b. Analyzing our financial values excludes how we feel about money.
    c. Financial values analysis omits why we feel as we do about money.
    d. Once we analyze financial goals and values, results will not change.

45. Which of the following is the most accurate definition of opportunity cost?
    a. What you get from giving up something else
    b. What you have to give up to get something
    c. An exchange, always measurable as money
    d. The dollar price to buy a specific opportunity

46. The law requires food labels to include which of the following information?
    a. Product name, form, amount, name and address, and ingredients
    b. The product name is required, but not the address of the company
    c. The weight or fluid ounces must be listed, but not every ingredient
    d. All ingredients must be listed, but weight or fluid ounces is optional

47. Currently, US laws mandate Nutrition Facts panels on food packaging for:
    a. All foods being sold.
    b. Most foods but not all of them.
    c. Foods making nutritional or health claims.
    d. No foods; it is recommended but not mandatory.

48. In management decision-making, managers may evaluate alternatives according to four parameters. Determining whether a company's performance goals can maintain a particular alternative or not reflects which of these parameters?
    a. Whether an alternative is legal
    b. Whether an alternative is ethical
    c. Whether an alternative is practical
    d. Whether an alternative is economical

49. Which of the following is a *disadvantage* of group decision-making?
    a. Group decision-making can reduce cognitive biases.
    b. Group decision-making combines skills and abilities.
    c. Group decision-making always prevents agreement.
    d. Group decision-making work can lead to group think.

50. In prioritizing as a time management technique, in which order should tasks be done?
    a. Urgent tasks first, then the important tasks next
    b. Important tasks first, then the urgent tasks next
    c. Urgent important tasks first, then the important
    d. First the urgent tasks, then the urgent important

51. For trustworthy online sources of quality health information, what is NOT recommended by the FTC?
    a. Websites of federal government agencies
    b. Disease-specific nonprofit group websites
    c. Search engine results on any health topics
    d. Medical school and/or university websites

52. Which of the following is true about finding child care services?
    a. Family-run day cares and traditional facilities charge about the same.
    b. Websites like SitterCity.com often charge more than nanny agencies.
    c. Compatibility between families is the only caveat with nanny-sharing.
    d. Babysitting co-ops are better choices for parents who work part-time.

53. Of the following smartphone apps for finding repair services, which is/are NOT really free?
    a. The apps from Yelp and Yellow Pages
    b. Angie's List, Find Home Services apps
    c. Redbeacon Home Services, RepairPal
    d. Home Improvement and Remodeling

54. When shopping for a car, which of the following should consumers consider most?
    a. The car's appearance
    b. The car's brand name
    c. The car's performance
    d. The car's planned uses

55. Which of the following is true about people's nutritional requirements?
    a. Drinking tea or coffee does not affect a person's nutritional requirements.
    b. Individual requirements for vitamin D are not affected by where one lives.
    c. People who exercise more need more food, but may metabolize it better.
    d. Malnutrition is only found to be a problem in today's developing countries.

56. Which of the following populations has a lower dietary requirement for iron?
    a. Vegetarians
    b. Young children
    c. Pregnant women
    d. Postmenopausal women

57. As adults get older, they are *most* likely to have poorer absorption from foods of which vitamin?
    a. Vitamin A
    b. Vitamin C
    c. Vitamin B_{12}
    d. Vitamin E

58. Which of the following foods is a source of the most vitamin A?
    a. Sweet potatoes
    b. Animal livers
    c. Carrots
    d. Kale

59. Which vitamins are water-soluble, so a body can have too little but not too much of them?
    a. Just vitamin C
    b. All B vitamins
    c. None of these
    d. All of these are

60. What is true about the USDA's Food Pyramid?
    a. MyPyramid was replaced by MyPlate by the USDA in 2011.
    b. MyPyramid is the current government food group symbol.
    c. MyPyramid and MyPlate both have the same food groups.
    d. MyPyramid had fewer food groups than MyPlate includes.

61. The values of nutrients on food and supplement labels developed by the FDA are currently called:
    a. RDAs
    b. DVs
    c. AIs
    d. UIs

62. Obesity is correlated with which of the following health conditions?
    a. Diabetes
    b. Hypertension
    c. All these and more
    d. Hypercholesterolemia

63. In which eating disorder is the patient more likely to retain a normal body weight?
    a. Neither of these
    b. Both of these
    c. Anorexia
    d. Bulimia

64. Which of the following religions formally prohibit(s) eating pork?
    a. Islam
    b. Judaism
    c. (A) and (B)
    d. Buddhism

65. What do nutrition experts recommend to most people for healthy eating and weight control?
    a. Multitasking, i.e., eating while working, driving, etc., aids in losing weight.
    b. The kinds of foods people eat are what matter rather than the amounts.
    c. When trying to lose weight, people should weigh themselves every day.
    d. Most people need to change their lifestyles for permanent weight loss.

66. Among eight main goals of planning a menu, which two are reflected in considering whether there will be leftovers that can be reused, and whether the meal smells and tastes good?
    a. Presentation and meal service
    b. Managing time and nutrition
    c. Satiety and food practicality
    d. Economics and palatability

67. Which of the following represents good dining etiquette at a dinner party?
    a. Only giving an RSVP if one will not attend
    b. Asking what food the hosts will be serving
    c. Asking what dress is suitable when invited
    d. Beginning to eat as soon as one sits down

68. Of the following, which food preparation(s) is/are LEAST likely to cause food-borne illnesses?
    a. Improperly canned or fermented
    b. Uncooked, i.e., raw meats/produce
    c. Undercooked, i.e., not long enough
    d. Overcooked, i.e., cooking too long

69. What can cause some kinds of dough to become tough?
    a. Overhandling any fat-based pastry or cookie dough
    b. Pinching buttery pastry edges with warm fingers
    c. Overhandling candy clay made using chocolate
    d. Putting very wet filling into a pie crust dough

70. Which of the following food additives is the safest to consume?
    a. Sodium pectinate
    b. Sodium bisulfite
    c. Sodium nitrate
    d. Sodium nitrite

71. What is true about how you can tell if yeast is still active after long-term storage?
    a. There is no way to test yeast, so you should not store it too long.
    b. The only way to tell is to use it in a recipe and see what happens.
    c. "Quick-rising" yeast can be "proofed" the same as regular yeast.
    d. To "proof" regular yeast, add warm water; then wait 10 minutes.

72. According to wardrobe experts, which is most accurate about women's wearing habits?
    a. Most women tend to wear fewer than half the clothes they buy.
    b. Most women tend to wear nearly all of the clothes that they buy.
    c. Most women tend to wear over half of the clothes that they buy.
    d. Most women tend to wear varying amounts of clothes they buy.

73. What is the best way to sort clothing in the closet to find items and assemble outfits easily?
    a. Sort first by colors, and then sort second by category.
    b. Sort by placing favorite items to be most within reach.
    c. Sort by placing item types wherever they will fit best.
    d. Sort first by category, and then sort second by colors.

74. Color analysts often categorize individuals' most flattering color palettes by skin tone into the four seasons. Which of the following represents typically good colors for someone who is a "winter"?
    a. Yellows, oranges, browns, earth tones
    b. Blues, greens, purples, black, and white
    c. Light, soft pastel tints of all/most colors
    d. Bright, vibrant primary/secondary hues

75. Which types of fabric are usually most flattering to an overweight body type?
    a. Medium-weight fabrics with a flat texture
    b. Soft, fine-gauge knits with a cuddly texture
    c. Strong, large-gauge knits with nubby texture
    d. Smooth, very shiny fabrics like silk or silk-look

76. Of the following fabrics, which one is NOT made using a plain weave?
    a. Denim
    b. Muslin
    c. Percale
    d. Burlap

77. In textile manufacturing, what is the most accurate definition of the term "gray goods"?
    a. Fabrics that have not been dyed
    b. Unfinished knit or woven fabrics
    c. Fabrics that are not bleached yet
    d. Any textile that is gray in its color

78. Which of the following fabric care symbols on a garment means it should be dry cleaned?
    a. A triangle shape
    b. A circular shape
    c. A square shape
    d. A circle in a square

79. In planning for buying a house, what do realtors recommend the buyer should do first?
    a. Determine if they can afford down payment, closing costs, monthly payment
    b. Determine in advance that their credit will be good enough to get a good loan
    c. Determine what they need and want, and when, in their real estate purchase
    d. Determine all of these things at the same time; the sequence does not matter

80. When a consumer hires a realtor to help in buying a home, which information that the realtor gives the consumer is most important for the realtor to update regularly?
    a. The current market conditions
    b. Various options for financing
    c. All these should be updated
    d. Specific negotiating methods

81. What is the primary consideration in real estate financing for home buyers?
    a. Obtaining a mortgage loan
    b. A loan with the best terms
    c. A loan that costs the least
    d. (B) and (C) rather than (A)

82. What is best for consumers to do when they want to buy a house?
    a. Look at homes in the location(s) they prefer the most
    b. Let a realtor suggest properties based on their needs
    c. They may do one or all of these things as they choose.
    d. Look at listings for homes with prices they can afford

83. Lenders generally require mortgages to be guaranteed by outside third parties (e.g., the FHA, VA, or a private mortgage insurer [PMI]) if the home buyer makes a less than ___ down payment.
    a. 20%
    b. 10%
    c. 50%
    d. 30%

84. Which of the following forms of insurance related to owning a home covers the loss of personal property in the home?
    a. Title insurance
    b. Flood insurance
    c. Home warranties
    d. Homeowners' only

85. Housing meets human physical, psychological, and social and cultural needs. Which of the following represents how housing meets social needs?
    a. By providing a sense of privacy and of personal space
    b. By providing a communal space for the human family
    c. By providing shelter from weather and giving security
    d. By providing all these, which all represent social needs

86. Which of the following elements most makes the floor plan of a house effective?
    a. How people move through it
    b. How people use the hallways
    c. How it looks from standing up
    d. How it looks from sitting down

87. In a home designed for a family, which rooms should be farthest apart from each other?
    a. Master bedroom and playroom
    b. The kitchen and the family room
    c. The family room and dining room
    d. Master bedroom from bedrooms

88. Which of the following solutions would be most practical in housing for a family?
    a. Moving to other houses as children grow older
    b. Remodeling the house as family needs change
    c. A house having some rooms with flexible uses
    d. Parents get an apartment when children move

89. Historically, family and consumer sciences began in:
    a. 1909
    b. 1910
    c. 1899
    d. 1926

90. Who founded the American Association of Family and Consumer Sciences?
    a. Mildred Chamberlain
    b. Elizabeth C. Stanton
    c. Susan B. Anthony
    d. Ellen H. Richards

91. What is most accurate about Family and Consumer Sciences in America?
    a. It is a course students are required to take in most high schools.
    b. It satisfies the credit in Sciences for graduation in most high schools.
    c. It satisfies the Humanities credit for graduation in most high schools.
    d. It is a course that is elective for students in most middle schools.

92. The ultimate and overall goal of professionals in FCS is to help people improve their quality of living:
    a. By applying their skills to everyday life.
    b. By working as educators to instruct them.
    c. By improving consumer goods and services.
    d. By helping them make informed decisions.

93. Before the home economics movement began, who of the following pioneered domestic sciences?
    a. Both Catherine Beecher and Harriet Beecher Stowe did this.
    b. Educator Catherine Beecher, sister of Harriet Beecher Stowe
    c. *Uncle Tom's Cabin* author and activist, Harriet Beecher Stowe
    d. Neither Catherine Beecher nor Harriet Beecher Stowe did this.

94. Which of the following is true about the relationship of gender stereotypes to laws and policies?
    a. Stereotypes are attitudes, but they never attain any legal status.
    b. Stereotypes often become laws when legislation supports them.
    c. Stereotypes contributing to laws for good intentions do no harm.
    d. Stereotypes that influence laws only discriminate against women.

95. Home economics has been identified as crucially instrumental in America's transition from 19th-century "domesticity" to 20th-century "modernity" (Cornell University). Which activities of late-1800s home economists were responsible for accomplishing this change?
    a. Focusing on research into the science of child development
    b. Focusing on research into science and principles of nutrition
    c. Focusing on and furthering civil and equal rights movements
    d. Focusing on the organization and design of American homes

96. What should students taking occupational family and consumer sciences courses mainly be learning?
    a. How to prepare themselves for becoming homeowners
    b. How to prepare themselves for careers on a lifelong basis
    c. How to prepare themselves for getting paid employment
    d. How to prepare themselves for balancing family and work

97. To which of the National Standards for Family and Consumer Sciences does the competency of analyzing how career decisions can affect the balance between family life and work belong?
    a. Career, Community, and Family Connections
    b. Consumer and Family Resources
    c. Family and Community Services
    d. Consumer Services

98. Under National Standards for Family and Consumer Sciences Area of Study 5.0, Facilities Management and Maintenance, Content Standard 5.2 is: "Demonstrate planning, organizing, and maintaining an efficient housekeeping operation for residential or commercial facilities." Which of the following is one of the competencies included under this Content Standard?
    a. "Demonstrate a waste minimization plan."
    b. "Analyze energy efficient methods."
    c. "Design energy efficient methods."
    d. "Apply security procedures."

99. In the Family and Consumer Sciences National Standards, under Area of Study 9.0, Food Science, Dietetics, and Nutrition, which of the following is a competency under Content Standard 9.2, "Apply risk management procedures to food safety, food testing, and sanitation"?
    a. "Apply principles of food production to maximize nutrient retention in prepared foods."
    b. "Design instruction on nutrition for health maintenance and disease prevention."
    c. "Demonstrate standard procedures for receiving and storage of raw and prepared foods."
    d. "Establish par levels for the purchase of supplies based on an organization's needs."

100. Housing and Interior Design is Area of Study 11.0 of the National Standards for Family and Consumer Sciences. In this area, Content Standard 11.3 is "Apply housing and interior design knowledge, skills, and processes to meet specific design needs." Of the following competencies, which one falls under this Content Standard?
    a. "Critique design plans to address client's needs, goals, and resources.
    b. "Describe features of furnishings that are characteristic of various historical periods."
    c. "Demonstrate measuring, estimating, ordering, purchasing, pricing, and repurposing skills."
    d. "Demonstrate procedures for reporting and handling accidents, safety, and security incidents."

101. The National Standards for Family and Consumer Sciences include Interpersonal Relationships, which is Area of Study 13.0. This area includes the following competency: "Apply critical thinking and ethical standards when making judgments and taking action." Under which of the following Content Standards does this competency belong?
    a. 13.5: "Demonstrate teamwork and leadership skills in the family, workplace, and community."
    b. 13.6: "Demonstrate standards that guide behavior in interpersonal relationships."
    c. 13.3: "Demonstrate communication skills that contribute to positive relationships."
    d. 13.4: "Evaluate effective conflict prevention and management techniques."

102. In the National Standards for Family and Consumer Sciences Education, Parenting is Area of Study 15.0. One of the competencies in Parenting is: "Apply communication strategies that promote positive self-esteem in family members." This competency belongs under which Content Standard for Parenting?
    a. 15.4: "Analyze physical and emotional factors related to beginning the parenting process."
    b. 15.2: "Evaluate parenting practices that maximize human growth and development."
    c. 15.3: "Evaluate external support systems that provide services for parents."
    d. 15.1: "Analyze roles and responsibilities of parenting."

103. Which of the following is NOT a purpose or outcome of the laboratory method of instruction?
    a. Students gain motivation through their hands-on experience in the lab.
    b. Students gain opportunities for direct participation in original research.
    c. Students gain skills in using the laboratory equipment and instruments.
    d. Students gain the ability to take lecture notes in the form of an outline.

104. In the demonstration method of instruction, which of the following steps comes last?
    a. Conclusion
    b. Evaluation
    c. Introduction
    d. Development

105. Someone tells a joke to a group of people, and following the punch line is complete silence. To which component of the communication process does this relate most?
    a. Encoding
    b. Feedback
    c. Decoding
    d. Medium

106. In applying the Leadership Process Model (Dunham and Pierce, 1989), to which of the following principles in this model does a leader's actively building trust with team members relate most?
    a. Focusing on relationship development
    b. Being aware of actions and reactions
    c. Leading honestly and ethically
    d. Consciously assigning tasks

107. The Family, Career and Community Leaders of America (FCCLA) has a mission to use Family and Consumer Sciences education to further personal growth and development in students. Its members develop life skills focused on several roles. Which of the following is NOT one of these roles?
    a. Wage earners
    b. Family members
    c. Business owners
    d. Community leaders

- 18 -

108. In terms of career education, the AAFCS's Education Fundamentals certification can help recipients gain jobs and continuing education in which kinds of careers?
    a. Public school systems but not private schools
    b. Corporate businesses and nonprofits equally
    c. School systems rather than higher education
    d. At schools more than after-school programs

109. Some researchers investigating how teachers of Family and Consumer Sciences have been adopting technology in their instructional practices have found which of the following factors most influential?
    a. The ages of teachers
    b. Technology availability
    c. Anxiety about technology
    d. Technology integration barriers

110. Which is true about integrating FCS with other academic areas of the curriculum?
    a. Historically, curricular deficits developed from the separation of academic and vocational courses.
    b. Historically, curricular deficits developed from the separation of college/non-college preparations.
    c. Regarding integration of FCS and other CTE courses with academics in curriculum, these are all true.
    d. Many State Common Core Standards now integrate career and technical education with academics.

111. Of the following, which best reflects a principle of effective classroom management?
    a. Classroom management should address only disruptive, not off-task behaviors.
    b. Classroom management should teach students to manage their own behaviors.
    c. Classroom management is only needed if things take on-task students off-task.
    d. Classroom management need not teach students to be on-task, which is normal.

112. Which of the following is accurate regarding future careers for FCS majors?
    a. Accelerating social change causes stress, reducing need for human services administration.
    b. Jobs in wellness, long-term health care administration, and dependent care remain stable.
    c. More employment opportunities are now developing in the appliance and food industries.
    d. There is currently a decrease in the hotel, motel, travel, tourism, and restaurant industries.

113. Regarding financial institutions, what is the current status of careers for FCS graduates?
    a. Brokerage firms want to hire qualified financial planners, who are among FCS graduates.
    b. Banks and savings and loan associations are not presently accepting many job applicants.
    c. FCS financial planners are needed at insurance companies but not at counseling agencies.
    d. FCS financial planners need not understand community relationship and family dynamics.

114. For a FCS graduate who wants a career in marketing consumer products and services, which of the following represents one of the job descriptions they may perform?
    a. Giving personal nutrition, parenting, and financial counseling services
    b. Conducting market surveys to discover consumer habits and interests
    c. Bettering the design of consumer products or services in laboratories
    d. Implementing plans for the marketing of consumer goods or services

115. Which statement is most appropriate for students to develop career goals?
    a. Students should not consider preference but what they can do.
    b. Students should pursue the most available jobs, not what they like.
    c. Students should first list occupations, and then select their favorites.
    d. Students should list activities they enjoy most and pick one favorite.

116. Of the following, which is something that a job applicant should do for an interview?
    a. Sit rigidly on the edge of the chair rather than slouching in the seat.
    b. Chewing gum is okay, but only smoke if invited by the interviewer.
    c. Ask the interviewer initially what the job's salary and benefits are.
    d. Be prepared for typical interview questions whether asked or not.

117. Regarding good body language during job interviews, conversations, and other interactions, which of these should one do with one's hands?
    a. Use them to play with your hair or bite nails to appear natural.
    b. Use them not at all, clasping them or clenching fists if needed.
    c. Use them for making large, broad, and sweeping movements.
    d. Use them when speaking in a confident, relaxed, natural way.

118. Which of the following reflects one of the core values of the AAFCS Code of Ethics?
    a. To believe that individuals are the basic units of society
    b. To espouse variety in scholarship and lifetime learning
    c. To maintain the status quo and avoid frequent changes
    d. To compartmentalize approaches to supporting others

119. Under the AAFCS's Code of Ethics, its Statement of Principles of Professional Practice includes that members eschew practices that exploit, intimidate, or harm others, and that they maintain their profession's credibility. In which category of principles are these found?
    a. Integrity
    b. Confidentiality
    c. Conflict of Interest
    d. Professional Competence

120. Under the Integrity principle of the AAFCS Statement of Principles of Professional Practice in its Code of Ethics, which of the following behaviors is included?
    a. Avoiding division of loyalties or the appearance of them
    b. Avoiding disclosures of private information about others
    c. Avoiding practices outside the law and their qualifications
    d. Avoiding communications that are incorrect or misleading

Answers and Explanations

1. B: This is defined as an extended family because a grandparent lives with the parents and children. A nuclear family (A) is defined as only the parents and children living together. A blended family (C) is formed when two parents, each with children from a previous marriage or relationship, marry each other and both sets of children live together with both parents. A combined family (D) is not a commonly used term, but may be used as a synonym for a blended family.

2. D: First-born children tend to grow up being responsible and dependable because parents tend to have higher expectations of their first child and give them more responsibility. Middle children (A) tend to feel less pressure as their parents have more experience with parenting by the time they have them. Parents also tend to expect less from their second children (B) and focus less attention on them than first-borns. Parents often give more special attention to their youngest children (C), but also expect less of them.

3. B: Upper-middle-class families today are more likely to relocate for employment opportunities (e.g., college professors who must move to another university to accept a particular teaching and/or research position they want and are offered; or business professionals whose promotions require relocation, etc.), whereas lower-middle-class families (A), middle-class families (C), and lower-class families (D) are more likely to reside in places where some of their relatives live; and if they move, are more likely to move to other places where they also have relatives living.

4. B: Currently, existing laws do not recognize stepparents as parents of the children whose parents they marry. Hence, in order to have legal parental rights to their new spouses' children, stepparents must legally adopt those children. If a parent and stepparent get divorced (and the stepparent has not adopted to gain legal parental status), the law does not grant any visitation rights to the ex-stepparent (C). Current U.S. law uniformly does not recognize stepparents as legal parents. Thus, it is not true that the law is unclear; and stepparent rights to custody or visitation of ex-stepchildren are not decided case by case (D), but do not legally exist.

5. A: When a parent is widowed or divorced, younger children can be more likely to feel the effects of changes to their usual routines (B) and of the way that their remaining parent copes with the loss (C) than of the death or departure of one parent, rather than vice versa (D). Toddlers may fear losing the other parent as well, so that parent must give them plenty of reassurance and feelings of security.

6. A: In stages of family development, the Parental stage consists of three parts: expanding, developing, and launching. When couples first marry, they share many activities. After they have children in the expanding years (A), the time they have to share activities as a couple is dramatically decreased. During the developing years (B) of the parental stage, children begin school: while families have limited time and more activities take place outside of the home, family members typically manage and share their duties successfully. In the launching years (C), children become independent, signaling the end of the parental stage of family development. After their children move out, "empty nest" parents return to being couples and having more time to share activities during their middle years (D).

7. B: According to some family life stage models (cf. Carter & McGoldrick, 1999; Carr, 2006), the stage of "family of origin experiences" involves primary developmental tasks of maintaining relationships with parents, siblings, and peers; completing one's education; and establishing

foundations for a model of family life, which children rely on as adults to form their own families. The second stage is leaving the home (A), with primary tasks of differentiation of self from family; establishing adult-to-adult relationships with parents; forming intimate relationships with peers; starting to work, developing a work identity, and becoming financially independent. The third stage is the "premarriage stage" (D), with primary tasks of choosing a life partner; developing the couple's relationship; and deciding to create a home with the partner. The fourth stage is the "childless couple stage" (C), with primary tasks of learning, emotionally and practically, to live with a partner; and adjusting family of origin relationships to include the partner. (This model includes four more subsequent stages.)

8. D: American society today encompasses so many and diverse versions of families that stage theories of family development often do not describe them adequately. Families may progress through stages out of their usual sequence, or revisit some stages when parents remarry after being widowed or divorced. This reflects a disadvantage of stage theories, which describe more normative or typical family stages. That the stages in these theories express the typical foremost concerns of families in each stage (A) is an advantage of stage theories (for example, referring to an "infant and toddler" stage evokes health, safety, and protection concerns; labeling periods of childhood as "teething", "toileting," or "tantrum" stages instantly evokes the family's main focus). Providing convenient common vocabularies (B) for describing family development is another advantage of stage theories. Systems theories focus more on less linear family dynamics and family responses to change, whereas stage theories focus more on sequential phases of family development (C).

9. C: Piaget's later Preoperational stage, when children's thinking becomes less egocentric but still retains animistic and magical characteristics, takes place during the preschool years (ages c. 3–6 years). This corresponds to Duvall's family development stage of Families with Preschoolers, when parents must adapt to the needs of young children and cope with young children's intrusions on their privacy and the energy drain of caring for and supervising preschoolers. Duvall described choice (A) as tasks of her Families with School-Age Children stage; (B) as tasks of her Families with Teenagers stage; and (D) as tasks of her Families with Infants stage.

10. A: Bowlby defined a secure base as the parent or attachment figure, who provides a constant source of security, functioning as the young child's "base" like a base camp or headquarters. Having this secure base enables the child to venture forth to explore the environment with the knowledge that s/he can still return to the base for security rather than lose his/her way. Bowlby defined the safe haven (B) as the child's being able to return to the parent to regain safety and comfort when s/he encounters a threat or feels fear. Bowlby defined separation distress (C) as the anxiety felt by young children when the parent is not there. He defined proximity maintenance (D) as the child's need to be near the parent, and in general the human being's desire to be near other people to whom s/he is attached.

11. C: The parenting dimension labeled by Baumrind as "clarity of communication" involves how wiling parents are to ask for their children's opinions and reason with them to encourage the behaviors they want as parts of communicating with their children. Nurturance (A) is what Baumrind named the dimension involving parents' protecting their children's physical and emotional welfare and expressing approval and warmth toward their children. Parental control (B) is Baumrind's label for the dimension wherein parents enforce rules for behavior with their children. Maturity demands (D) are what Baumrind described as the dimension of expectations parents have for their children to behave up to their abilities.

12. C: Baumrind and other researchers applying her theory of parenting styles have found that the authoritarian style, which features rigid rules and insistence on obedience; a lack of warmth; a tendency to punish children physically, insult them verbally, and/or withdraw approval or love to coerce them to conform, tends to produce children who are well-behaved but anxious, moody, and more likely to follow than to lead. Independent, responsible, high-achieving children (A) are likely to be the products of the authoritative parenting style. Immature, irresponsible, impulse-ridden (B) children are likely to be the products of the permissive (also called permissive-indulgent) parenting style. Depressed, low-functioning children who tend toward delinquency (D) are likely to be the products of the uninvolved (also called permissive-uninvolved) parenting style.

13. C: Schaefer conceived of parenting styles as existing across two dimensions: (1) along a continuum from love to hostility, and along a continuum from autonomy to control. For example, parents who give much love and much autonomy tend to be permissive and produce impulsive children; parents who give more love but also more control tend to produce children who are well-behaved but not very independent; parents who are hostile and controlling produce fearful and/or rebellious children; parents with high hostility and low control reject and/or neglect children, producing dysfunctional individuals.

14. A: Bandura discovered that children learn not only from experiencing the consequences of their own behaviors (B), but can also learn vicariously by observing others' behaviors and their consequences, and then imitating those behaviors to obtain similar rewards or avoid similar punishments. In his social learning theory, Bandura proposed that children do indeed learn from observing and imitating others' behaviors (C). The concept that children learn better from positive reinforcement than from punishment (D) is a principle of behaviorism. Bandura's theory uses behaviorist concepts, but adds to behaviorism's idea that learning occurs through environmental consequences of behaviors the social element of observing others' behaviors and their consequences and then imitating them. (Behaviorists have found punishments induce unfavorable reactions threefold over rewards, but positive reinforcements [rewards] are also far more powerful in encouraging desired behaviors than punishments in discouraging undesired behaviors.)

15. C: Bandura conducted landmark experiments wherein children watched video with violent behavioral content and found that the children did display an increase in aggressive behaviors after viewing, confirming Bandura's theory of observational learning. An additional concern with young children is that they often cannot distinguish reality from fantasy (A), but this does not mean their behavior is unaffected. It can more often mean they cannot understand or predict real outcomes; like that hitting others can hurt them. (For example, a child who sees a cartoon character blown up and then fine immediately thereafter might think this can happen in reality.) Children were found to imitate both aggressive and altruistic behaviors they observed (B). While some young children certainly reacted fearfully to video violence, the fact still remains that children did display more aggressive behaviors after viewing video violence (D) in Bandura's studies.

16. B: In Maslow's hierarchy of needs, the bottom of the pyramid represents needs that take priority because they are required for survival. Hence making sure that children get enough food and sleep is ranked by Maslow among his first level, Physiological needs. Maslow's hierarchy is progressive: each needs level must be met before a person can ascend to the next. After meeting physiological needs, the second level is Security needs; for parents this includes ensuring their children have adequate shelter and safety (C). The third level is Social needs; for parents, this includes giving children love, affection, and a sense of belonging (A). The fourth level is Esteem needs; to meet these, parents build high self-esteem and feelings of personal worth (D) in their

children. (The fifth level at the top of the pyramid is Self-Actualization Needs, i.e., to fulfill one's fullest potential, after meeting all other needs.)

17. D: Family lifestyle is a factor affecting family relationships that includes such elements as communication styles, eating habits, and kinds of friends of the family members. Family structure (A) includes such examples as single-parent families, blended families with stepparents, two-parent families, and extended families. Family resources (B) include such things as how much money the family has, how much time, how much education, how many friends, social support networks, etc. Family roles (C) encompass both basic roles, such as parent, child, sibling, and grandparent; and other roles family members adopt like troublemaker, peacemaker, clown, disciplinarian, etc.

18. B: One benefit of family recreation to individual family members is that it can teach members of the family skills that they will use for the rest of their lives. Benefits of family recreation to the family unit as a whole include improved communication within the family (A), increased stability of the family and of interactions within it (C), and a way to maintain family relationships (D), among others.

19. C: Erikson's stage of Initiative vs. Guilt occurs during the preschool years of early childhood, when children begin exploring their environments, first develop awareness of the different social roles existing around them, and experience feelings of either purpose and accomplishment or guilt and inhibition. Erikson identified the family as the primary influence on children's development during this stage. Trust vs. Mistrust (A) occurs during infancy, when a baby's needs are either met fully and consistently, engendering feelings that the world can be trusted; or incompletely and/or inconsistently, fostering a general mistrust of people. Industry vs. Inferiority (B) occurs when children start school, their world widens from the family to school and social relationships, and they develop a sense of either mastery or inadequacy.

20. C: Gesell described 10-year-old children as viewing their parents' word as law and wholeheartedly accepting their parents without reservations. He described 8-year-olds (A) as demanding an understanding and close relationship with parents, particularly their mothers. He described 6-year-olds (B) as demoting their mothers from the center of their world to taking second place to themselves, as they now want to be the center of their own world at this age and tend to blame their mothers for whatever is wrong at the time. Gesell described 9-year-olds (D) as becoming more interested in friends and their opinions than in family and their opinions, resisting parental direction, and withdrawing from their family circles as much as they can in favor of independence and self-sufficiency.

21. C: Havighurst identified developmental tasks in each of the six stages of human development he defined. Learning to walk, talk, eat, eliminate, stabilize physically; sexual modesty and differences, simple physical and social reality concepts, right and wrong; developing a conscience, and learning to relate the self emotionally to parents and siblings are tasks he assigned to the period from birth to 6 years. He identified learning of basic reading, writing, and calculation skills; physical game skills, getting along with peers; developing everyday living concepts, morality, values, personal independence, a gender role, healthy self-attitudes, and attitudes toward institutions and social groups as tasks for those from 6 to 12 years (A). He included tasks in pre-teen and teen years (B) as maturing peer relations; emotional independence from adults; career preparation and choice; marriage and family life preparation; developing concepts and skills for civic competence; developing social responsibility and an ethical system, etc. Among tasks of early adulthood (D), Havighurst included marrying, starting families, raising children, managing households, beginning careers, etc.

22. A: Piaget used the term anomy to mean that a child's social and moral development was not regulated, either by the self or by others. He used the term heteronomy to mean regulation of this development by others, and autonomy to mean regulation by the self. He characterized social and moral development in children as progressing from anomy (no regulation) to heteronomy (regulation by adults) to autonomy (self-regulation).

23. D: The most basic level of needs is physiological—for water, sleep, food, elimination, etc.—and comes first in Maslow's hierarchy. These are the needs most important to a newborn infant. Maslow's second level of needs is of those for safety and security (B), which become more important to toddlers. His third level is of needs for love and belonging (A), which become important as children grow. As they get older, they also have needs on Maslow's fourth level, for esteem, i.e., respect, self-confidence, and achievement. His fifth and most evolved level is of needs for self-actualization (C), which includes problem-solving, creativity, moral and ethical development, accepting the truth, and realizing one's greatest potentials. (Note: Maslow's needs levels do not depend only on age; adults may experience any level as a priority at any time in life. However, infants are not yet cognitively developed enough to be concerned with the higher levels.)

24. C: Infancy, i.e., birth to 2 years, is a life stage that includes developmental tasks of cognitively understanding simple causality, the nature of objects, and categorization as well as early emotional development, social attachment; maturation in motor, perceptual, and sensory functions, etc. Toddlerhood (A) includes developmental tasks of self-control, language, elaborated locomotion, pretend play, etc. Early school ages (B) include developmental tasks of group play, gender role identification, early moral development, etc. Middle school ages (D) include tasks of performing concrete mental operations; learning skills; self-evaluation; developing friendships; playing on teams, etc.

25. A: Conservation of amount, i.e., understanding that there is the same amount of a substance even if its shape, appearance, or arrangement is changed, is a typical developmental task for children at the middle school ages, e.g., around six to twelve years old. This is a part of what Piaget called Concrete Operations, which children at the earliest school ages (e.g., around four to six years old) typically cannot yet understand or perform. Typical developmental tasks for these younger school-age children include identifying with female or male sex roles (B), developing early concepts of basic morality (C), and learning to play in groups (D) with other children.

26. B: In later adulthood, e.g., around 60 to 75 years, it is a common developmental task to redirect one's energies to new activities and roles as life circumstances change. Common developmental tasks in middle adulthood (A), e.g., around ages between 34 and 60 years, include nurturing marital relationships, parenting, household management, and career management. Early adulthood (C), e.g., around 22 to 34 years old, includes developmental tasks like going to work, getting married, and having children. In old age (D), e.g., from age 75 to death, includes developmental tasks like coping with the physiological changes aging causes, making life reviews, and developing psychohistorical perspectives.

27. A: The primary area of development disabled by cerebral palsy is that of motor skills. Cerebral palsy impairs control and coordination of the nerves and muscles in motor movements. Individuals with cerebral palsy do not have impaired cognitive development (B) unless they have some co-existing intellectual disability. Their emotional development (C) and social skills development (D) are also not impaired by the cerebral palsy itself (though they must have access to equal

- 25 -

opportunities to develop these areas without such experiences being prevented by their physical disabilities).

28. B: Intellectual disability is most characterized by learning in the same way as nondisabled peers, but at an overall slower rate. The autism spectrum (A) is more characterized by normal intelligence and learning at a normal rate but with deficits in specific areas, e.g., in social comprehension, range of interests and activities, and verbal communication for some. Sensory impairments (C) do not necessarily cause slower overall learning: deaf children take longer to learn reading specifically because of its strong auditory basis, but they learn language just as quickly provided sign language or other accessible modalities; blind children, given Braille or other methods, do too; and neither deaf nor blind children learn more slowly in other areas. While those with learning disabilities (D) may or may not take longer to learn certain things, they are not intellectually disabled; moreover, they do *not* learn the same way as others, but learn differently in specific areas. They often succeed in these areas if taught differently.

29. D: What Bronfenbrenner termed the microsystem is a person's immediate environment, including family, friends, communities, religious groups, and others with which the person has direct contact and regular interactions. The exosystem (A) is what Bronfenbrenner named the wider social system of events and experiences that directly affect a person's microsystems but which the person does not construct; e.g., getting or losing a job. The mesosystem (B) is what Bronfenbrenner called the system of connections between elements of the microsystem; e.g., between a child's parents and teachers, friends and relatives, etc. The macrosystem (C) is what Bronfenbrenner labeled the cultural beliefs, values, laws, rules, and customs that influence the person. (Bronfenbrenner also identified the chronosystem, a system in the dimension of time that includes processes and events like biological maturation, parental death, etc.)

30. B: Freud proposed that like ancient Greek tragedian Sophocles's character Oedipus, who unwittingly murdered his father and married his mother, all boys experience a conflict in early childhood (often around ages 4 to 5) wherein they unconsciously desire their mothers and wish to eliminate their fathers as rivals for the mothers' affection. According to Freud, it was impossible for a boy not to have this conflict (A). He said that young boys resolve this conflict through "identification with the aggressor," i.e. wanting to be like the father and imitating him, thereby relieving guilt over their unacceptable sexual and aggressive impulses toward each respective parent. Perpetuating the conflict (C) was not a solution to Freud, but rather an unhealthy fixation that would undermine all relationships. Simply experiencing the conflict (D) was not sufficient in Freud's theory; it must also be successfully resolved.

31. D: According to Bowen's Family Systems Theory, differentiation of self, determined by family relationships during childhood and adolescence, is important to intrapersonal and interpersonal health. Individuals with poor differentiation of self are overly interdependent with others and overly dependent on approval and acceptance from others. Individuals with poorly differentiated selves may be either chameleons, always changing their behaviors and attitudes to agree and conform with others, please them, and gain their approval (A), or bullies who pressure others to conform and agree with what they decide is right (B). Both types of extremes in behavior indicate poor differentiation of self; therefore it is incorrect that neither of them fits the description (C).

32. B: Satir identified five common roles adopted by family members instead of their true identities, especially when under stress. Always blaming, criticizing, and finding fault with the others (A) is one such dysfunctional role. Another is always trying to please the others (C) and apologizing. A third is always distracting the others (D) to deflect their attention from emotional concerns. Hence

none of these is considered healthy and effective because family members use these behaviors out of low self-esteem to conceal what they are feeling. (A fifth category she described is the "computer," who outwardly denies all emotion in favor of intellectualizing.) According to Satir, only those she called "levelers," i.e., family members who communicate their true feelings honestly, directly, and openly, are interacting in a healthy and effective manner.

33. D: According to Hall, high-context communication is an indirect style of verbal communication. It uses a softer voice (A) and relies more on nonverbal behaviors (B) to express meaning. In contrast, low-context communication is clearer and more direct (C) and spoken in a firmer voice.

34. A: Interpreter-sensitive values are characteristic of high-context communication and mean the listener is expected to take responsibility for interpreting the speaker's meaning, much of which is conveyed through nonverbal behaviors (C), which the listener must "read between the lines" (D) to infer. Conversely, low-context communication uses sender-oriented values, meaning the speaker is expected to take responsibility for communicating clearly and directly (B) to make decoding simple (D) for the listener.

35. B: The gesture we call "thumbs up" is also used for hitchhiking in America, but not for hitchhiking in all other countries of the world (A). It does have different meanings in various countries. It means "zero" in France and coins or money in Japan; in Nigeria it is considered a rude gesture; when pumped up and down it is an obscene gesture in Australia, but means "one" in both Japan and Germany. Hence it does not have only one meaning in Japan (C). In America, it is not only a hitchhiking signal, but is also used to mean "okay" or "good job" or to express approval or support. Hence it does have multiple meanings in America (D).

36. B: Cooperative communication prevents conflict by suggesting rather than accusing; using "I" rather than "You"; and focusing on solving problems rather than focusing on the other person. Example (B) has these qualities. The examples in (A), (C), and (D) are all person-centered by accusing the other person of interrupting, not listening, etc.; whereas the example in (B) expresses the speaker's desires both to finish, and also to hear what the other person has to say. It also positively communicates the speaker's need to complete a message instead of negatively accusing the other person of not listening to it.

37. A: While Erikson based his theory on Freud's, one major difference between them is that Freud only included stages of development through adolescence, whereas Erikson included stages of development through old age until death. Freud considered the personality to be complete by adolescence, but Erikson viewed it as continuing to develop throughout life.

38. A: The Wall Street Reform and Consumer Protection Act of 2009, among other provisions, established the Office of Fair Lending and Equal Opportunity. The establishment of this office addresses the consumer's rights and responsibilities to redress (B), i.e., the right to request money or other benefits to compensate for a mistake made by a company and the responsibility to seek such compensation; and to choice (D), i.e., the right to a broad range of goods and services available at fair prices; and the responsibility to exercise care in choosing among these. Consumer rights and responsibilities to be heard (C) are addressed by protections for whistleblowers provided by the Consumer Financial Protection Agency, also established under the Wall Street Reform and Consumer Protection Act of 2009.

39. A: Making one's concerns heard to those who can address them is an example of the consumer's responsibility for being heard. Having one's voice heard about product development and

lawmaking (B) is an example of the consumer's *right* to be heard. Being able to choose among a variety of goods and services (C) is an example of the consumer's *right* to choice. An example of the consumer's *responsibility* for choice is to exercise due care and caution in choosing from among that variety. Accessing information that assures product statements are true (D) is an example of the consumer's *right* to information. An example of the consumer's *responsibility* regarding information is wisely conducting analyses and applications of the available product information.

40. B: The United Nations Guidelines for Consumer Protections (1985) include the right of consumers to a healthy environment. The Consumer Product Safety Commission (A) sets product safety standards, as do the Underwriters' Laboratories (C). The Bureau of Competition (D) protects investors who purchase tradable financial assets like bonds, stocks, etc., and helps provide that a wide selection of goods and services is available to consumers.

41. B: Research finds when consumers like the doctor they are seeing, they are less interested in considering price data for health care. However, when consumers have high out-of-pocket expenses (A) for health care, they are more interested in informing their decisions using price data. They are also more interested in the significance of price information when their medical conditions are not urgent (C) or serious because they have more time for health care comparison shopping. Consumers with few or no preconceptions about health care providers (D), e.g., through the influences of their own positive prior experiences, word-of-mouth communications, and/or advertising, are likewise more interested in using price data to inform their health care decisions.

42. C: The first thing consumers should do before making a decision to purchase goods or services is to identify their needs, e.g., how they will use the product or service; how often; where to store a product; the location of a service. The second thing they should do is to list the attributes they want the product or service to have (B); e.g., a doctor has long enough office visits, short enough patient waiting times, and a good bedside manner; an insurance company settles claims promptly, subrogates effectively, and charges low premiums; or a power tool is cordless, lightweight, and powerful. The third thing is to narrow the field of possible choices (A); e.g., which are available for sale, which have prices the consumer can afford; product support and customer service; and how each choice meets the consumer's needs and desired product/service attributes. Thus the order of these steps is not irrelevant (D).

43. D: The first step in financial planning is to determine what the individual's or family's current financial circumstances are. The second step is to develop what their financial goals will be (A). The third step is to identify different possible actions they may take (B). The fourth step is to evaluate the potential consequences of taking any of those actions among the alternatives (C). Additional steps include making a financial plan of action, implementing it, reevaluating that plan, and changing it as needed.

44. A: The reason we are advised to analyze our values regarding money and our financial goals is to help us distinguish between what we want and what we need. We may not have enough income for everything we want, but giving our true needs priority before spending on wants can help us stay within our budgets. Analyzing our financial values does include defining how we feel about money (B) and also why we feel as we do about it (C). The reason we are advised to conduct such analyses periodically is because once we have analyzed our financial goals and values, the results we get can still change over time (D): not only can the things we need and want change, but also the ways we feel about money and the reasons for those feelings can change with changes in life circumstances, personal maturity, etc.

45. B: The most accurate definition of opportunity cost is what you have to give up to get something else when they may be mutually exclusive financially. For example, someone may be able to attend school part-time while working full-time or work part-time while attending school full-time, or to do each of these part-time; but not to do both full-time. Opportunity cost is not the reverse (A); it represents something lost rather than something gained. While it represents a trade-off, such an exchange is NOT always measurable as amounts of money (C). The cost can be lost time, lost enjoyment, or any other usable benefit(s) lost by choosing an alternative. Opportunity cost does NOT refer to the dollar price of a specific opportunity (D) like college tuition, a mortgage, a car's sticker price, the price for season tickets, etc.

46. A: By law, food labels must include the name of the product (e.g. "chunk light tuna"), its form (e.g., "in spring water" or "in soybean oil"); its amount (i.e., weight in ounces, fluid ounces, pounds, grams, milligrams, etc.) (D); the name and address of the company (B) that packed, processed, or distributed the food; and every ingredient included in the food (C) must be listed as well.

47. B: At present, the FDA and USDA mandate that food packaging contain Nutrition Facts panels for most, but not all foods being sold (A). For example, single-ingredient packages of raw meats and poultry are not presently required to have Nutrition Facts panels on their labels, though the USDA has proposed this requirement before and has recently proposed it again. Foods containing nutritional or health claims (C) on their labels are included among those required to provide Nutrition Facts panels. Nutrition Facts panels are mandatory for most foods; hence (D) is incorrect.

48. D: Whether a company's performance goals can support an alternative reflects whether the alternative is economically feasible. Whether an alternative is legal (A) is reflected by whether an alternative is lawful in this country, and in others for companies that export goods or services. Whether it is ethical (B) is reflected if the alternative will not cause undue harm to stakeholders and is morally acceptable. Whether an alternative is practical (C) is reflected by whether the organization's management has the resources and abilities to implement it.

49. D: "Group think" is a disadvantage of group decision-making that happens when all the members of the group want so much to agree that they may unanimously adhere to the leader's idea, becoming blinded to alternative ideas. Each individual member is convinced by the power of the group as a whole that they must promote the given idea. Group think represents decision-making that is biased rather than objective. On the other hand, an advantage of group decision-making is that it can reduce the cognitive biases (A) that often exist more strongly in individually made decisions. Another advantage of group decision-making is that it benefits from the combined skills and abilities (B) of all group members. Always preventing agreement (C) would be a disadvantage of group decision-making if this were true; however, the facts that many management decisions are made in groups and that group think can occur prove that it is not true. Since agreement is often possible in group decision-making, (C) is not a valid disadvantage.

50. C: Urgent tasks need immediate attention, but are not necessarily important in the long term. Important tasks are significant in the long run; e.g., they help us attain our long-term goals and/or otherwise have meaningful consequences over time. Tasks that are both urgent and important will both precipitate crises if neglected, and also yield long-term benefits. Therefore, in prioritizing, one should complete all urgent important tasks first, and then concentrate on those tasks that are not urgent but are the most important. One needs to be able to identify whether tasks are urgent, important, or both and to what degree in order to prioritize them in this way.

51. C: For finding trustworthy online sources of reliable, current health information, the Federal Trade Commission (FTC) recommends visiting federal government agency websites (A), like http://www.nlm.nih.gov/medlineplus/, http://healthfinder.gov/, https://www.healthcare.gov/; http://www.cdc.gov/, http://medicare.gov/, www.fda.gov/consumer, http://www.cancer.gov/, www.nia.nih.gov, and http://womenshealth.gov/. Nonprofit groups focusing on specific diseases or conditions also provide reliable websites (B) offering research information and education to the public; these sites typically have .org extensions (though the FTC also warns consumers to beware phony .org sites set up by scammers). Websites run by medical schools and universities (D)—generally ending with .edu—or by reputable health facilities are also good sources. However, as the FTC points out and many of us have discovered on our own, the results we get from typing any given health topic into a search engine often include unreliable and/or outdated websites.

52. D: Babysitting co-ops involve several couples forming a group to rotate caring for each other's children. Each earns credits or points for care hours given, redeemed for their own children's care by other members. Or two sets of parents informally exchange a few care hours weekly with one another. These arrangements are easier for parents working part-time than those working full-time. Parents will find that family-run daycares, operated in providers' homes and often including providers' children, typically charge much less than traditional daycare facilities (A). Searching for child care on websites costs less than using nanny agencies (B), which can cost thousands in up-front charges; whereas charges on websites like SitterCity.com begin around $40 for membership. Families not only need compatibility in parenting practices and attitudes for nanny-sharing; an additional caveat (C) is if one family discontinues the service, leaving the other to scramble to locate another family to share or else pay the nanny's entire salary alone.

53. B: While iTunes lists the app from Angie's List as "Free", it also notes "***Membership required***". Angie's List once had free membership, but began charging several years ago; currently it costs $39.99 a year to join. Only paid members can download the app. The Find Home Services app costs $3.00. Many other apps are free, though: Yelp locates repair services including customer reviews as well as restaurants; its app is available for Android, iOS, and Windows phone systems. The Yellow Pages app is also free (A) and available for the same three systems. Redbeacon Home Services (a Home Depot subsidiary) and RepairPal for auto repair estimates and locating mechanics (C) are both free apps for iOS and Android systems. The Home Improvement and Remodeling (D) app for iOS and Android is free and lets consumers upload photos, connect with providers, receive quotes, and book services, all from their smartphones without meetings or even phone calls.

54. D: Many consumers care about the way a car looks (A), and some are loyal to particular brands (B) out of their previous good experiences with it; some want a car that has a powerful engine and handles well (C). While these may all be valid considerations for customer satisfaction, what consumers should consider most is how they plan to use the car. For example, if their daily work commute and weekend leisure trips all heavily involve stop-and-go traffic, an automatic transmission is a better choice than a manual one. People who frequently drive on bumpy, unpaved roads or in hilly areas may need a vehicle with front-wheel or four-wheel drive. Those who regularly drive long distances and are on budgets need good gas mileage; people driving with many children and pets need spacious interiors, etc. Choosing a car to fit the individual driver's needs and purposes is thus the most important factor of the choices named.

55. C: People who exercise more do need more calories from food since they burn more; however, exercise also enhances metabolic efficiency in some individuals. Drinking tea and/or coffee *does* affect nutritional requirements (A): both beverages interfere with the absorption of iron and zinc.

Vitamin D requirements *are* affected by where one lives (B): people living in the northern half of the United States do not get enough vitamin D through exposure to sunlight during winter. People living south of the 45th parallel, or a line drawn between Atlanta, Georgia, in the east and Los Angeles, California, in the west, have access to strong enough sunlight in winter for sufficient vitamin D, but often lack exposure to sunlight during summers when they stay indoors with air-conditioning to avoid the heat. Malnutrition is a serious problem in developing countries today, but is also an issue in developed countries (D) among people who eat too many overprocessed, refined foods whose nutrients have been removed.

56. D: Women of childbearing ages need to replace iron depleted monthly by menstrual blood loss. Postmenopausal women no longer lose blood through menstruation; hence their iron requirements are lower. Vegetarians (A) often require more iron because their diets lack animal proteins that provide sources of heme iron. Young children (B) need more iron (in proportion to their body weight) because they are growing rapidly. Pregnant women (C) need more iron to support their babies' proper development. (Insufficient iron can lead to infant mortality, low birth weight, premature birth, infant health problems, and delays in infant motor and cognitive functioning.)

57. C: Aging adults are most likely to have poorer absorption of vitamin B_{12} from foods because their stomachs produce less acid with aging, and stomach acid extracts this vitamin from the proteins containing it. Vitamins A (A), C (B), and E (D) are important to older adults for their antioxidant properties (antioxidants can prevent heart disease and some cancers, and may mitigate the process of aging), but aging is not known to decrease absorption of these from foods as it does with vitamin B_{12}.

58. B: Liver from any animal has the highest amount of vitamin A, with turkey liver being the highest, providing over 1500% of the Daily Value (DV) per 100-gram (3½-ounce) serving. Sweet potatoes (A) provide 384% of the DV of vitamin A per 100-gram serving. Carrots contain beta-carotene, which is converted by the body to vitamin A, providing 334% of the DV for a 100-gram (raw) serving. Kale (D) provides 308% of the DV of vitamin A per 100-gram serving via its carotenes.

59. D: Vitamin C (A) and all of the B-complex (B) vitamins (thiamine, riboflavin, niacin, pantothenic acid, pyridoxine, biotin, folic acid, and cobalamin) are water-soluble, meaning they can be dissolved in water. As such, they are not stored in the body's tissues; whatever the body cannot absorb is excreted in urine and perspiration. Hence one can have a deficiency of these vitamins, but not a surplus, and (C) is incorrect. (Fat-soluble vitamins are absorbed in fat and can be stored in the body tissues, where they can build up; so unlike with water-soluble vitamins, one can take in excessive fat-soluble vitamins [vitamins A, D, E, and K] that remain in the body.)

60. A: Although the "food pyramid" has long been familiar to most Americans (e.g., the USDA's former MyPyramid and also Mediterranean, Asian, and Latin American Diet Pyramids), the USDA actually replaced MyPyramid with MyPlate in June 2011. Hence the USDA refers to MyPlate as the current government food group symbol rather than MyPyramid (B). MyPlate does not have all of the same food groups as MyPyramid did (C): Whereas MyPyramid contained six food groups, MyPlate has only five because it does not include fats, oils, and sweets as MyPyramid did; hence MyPyramid had more food groups than MyPlate, not fewer (D). (MyPyramid advised "USE SPARINGLY" for this category; due to recent attention to the American obesity epidemic, however, the government decided to eliminate this category altogether as part of a healthful diet.)

61. B: Daily Values (DVs) are what the FDA currently uses on food and supplement labels to indicate the levels of nutrients in an average or standard serving of food related to approximately how much of each of them the average person needs. Recommended Dietary Allowances or RDAs (A) are what the FDA formerly used before the Dietary Supplement Health and Education Act (DSHEA, 1994) required supplements to show Supplement Facts on their labels. Adequate Intakes or AIs (C) are amounts of vitamins and minerals included in the reports called Dietary Reference Intakes (DRIs) issued by the Institute of Medicine. These reports also set the upper intake or UI (D) levels for vitamins and minerals. DVs, RDAs, and AIs frequently have the same values, but not always. DVs are the only ones on food and supplement labels, so they are what consumers should consider.

62. C: Obesity is correlated with diabetes (A); hypertension, i.e., high blood pressure (B); hypercholesterolemia, i.e., high cholesterol (D); heart disease; certain cancers; autoimmune diseases and other inflammatory conditions; and many other diseases and adverse health conditions.

63. D: In bulimia, the patient binge-eats abnormal amounts of food and then purges by vomiting, and may also abuse laxatives and/or diuretics. In anorexia (C), the patient starves, eating nothing or very little; and some anorexics also vomit and/or abuse laxatives and/or diuretics. However, bulimics typically eat more normal amounts of food outside of their secret binge-eating and purging sessions, so they usually retain more normal body weights and appearances (though they suffer electrolyte imbalances, erosion of the teeth's enamel, and other serious results of all the vomiting). In contrast, anorexics typically become severely underweight and appear emaciated as the disorder progresses because they never eat normal amounts of food.

64. C: Islam (A) and Judaism (B) formally prohibit eating pork, but Buddhism (D) overall does not. Some individual Buddhist sects prohibit eating any meat while others eat meat as a staple. One Buddhist sect prohibits its monks from eating certain kinds of meat, but does not ban any kinds of food for laypersons.

65. D: Nutrition experts advise people who want to lose weight permanently that they need to change their lifestyles rather than go on and off a diet, which results in regaining any weight lost. They also advise *against* eating while doing other things (A), which does not help in losing weight but more often leads to weight gain as people are not mindful of what and how much they eat or when they are full. While some kinds of foods are better for us than others, portion sizes *do* matter (B). Some foods, e.g., leafy greens, can be eaten in larger quantities than others, e.g., ice cream; but moderation in the amounts we eat overall is best. Experts advise people trying to lose or maintain weight to weigh themselves weekly, not daily (C). Normal daily weight fluctuations from fluids and other factors make true weights unclear; weighing weekly makes it easier to know whether one has lost, gained, or maintained weight.

66. D: Whether there will be leftovers that can be reused reflects the menu-planning goal of economics; whether the meal smells and tastes good reflects the goal of palatability. Presentation is reflected in atmosphere, table settings, etc.; meal service is reflected in choices like buffets, family service; Chinese, Russian, French, etc. (A). Time management is reflected in planning recipes that can be prepared and served in the time available (e.g.: Is food ready when guests are hungry? Can the host/ess sit and eat with guests, or is s/he busy with ongoing preparation and service most of the time they are eating?). Nutrition is reflected by whether courses or meal parts represent FDA food groups and proportions (B). Satiety is reflected in portion sizes, foods' nutrient content, and whether people feel satisfied after eating. Food practicality is reflected in whether foods in a menu

are available; convenient to find, store, and prepare; whether guests like them; and whether any are restricted from guests' diets for medical, religious, or other reasons (C).

67. C: It is considered acceptable etiquette when invited to a dinner party to ask what kind of dress is expected; however, it is *not* acceptable to ask what will be served (B). If a guest has dietary restrictions, it is politer to inform the hosts of these rather than to ask what foods they are serving. Etiquette dictates that it is courteous to RSVP to dinner party invitations both if attending and if not attending (A). Another rule of dining etiquette is that guests only begin to eat when the host/ess raises his/her fork (or spoon if the first course is soup), not as soon as they sit down to the table (D).

68. D: Cooking food for too long can burn it or dry it out, causing poor taste and texture and removing nutrients. Grilling or charring foods at high temperatures can cause it to contain carcinogens (cancer-promoting agents), as can burning them; but cancers are not food-borne illnesses, which are caused by viral, bacterial, or parasitic microorganisms present in foods. Improperly canned foods and fermented fish (A) can cause botulism, which can be deadly. Uncooked or raw meats and produce (B) can cause many food-borne illnesses, as can undercooked foods (C).

69. A: Any fat-based dough, e.g., for pie crusts, scones, cookies, or pastries, will become tough if handled too much. When making filled pastries using a buttery (fat-based) pastry dough, pinching the edges together with warm fingers (B) can make the dough too soft rather than tough. (Solutions are to chill the dough first, and handle it through a piece of plastic wrap.) Overhandling candy clay made with chocolate (C) will make it soften and melt rather than become tough. Putting very wet filling into pie crust (D) will make the dough soggy rather than tough, especially if the pie plate was not buttered or the dough was not brushed with egg white first.

70. A: Sodium pectinate, like pectin, is a safe carbohydrate added to fruits and vegetables to strengthen their cell walls and to jellies, jams, sauces, yogurts, and frostings as a gelling agent to thicken them. Sodium bisulfite (B) is safe for some people, though it destroys vitamin B_1; however, for individuals sensitive to it, particularly those with asthma, it can cause severe reactions and even death. It is used to prevent bacteria from growing in wines and keep certain foods from discoloring. Sodium nitrate (C) and sodium nitrite (D) are used in cured meats like hot dogs and bacon to preserve color and flavor and prevent bacterial growth, but are also associated with formation of carcinogenic (cancer-causing) nitrosamines. (Today, the addition of ascorbic acid or erythorbic acid mitigates nitrosamine formation, but nitrates and nitrites still present some risk. Also, these additives are mainly used in fatty, salty foods—another reason to avoid them.)

71. D: Regular active dry yeast can be stored 6 months to 1 year on a shelf or more than 1 year in the freezer. After this long, it is possible to test it, so (A) is incorrect. It is not necessary to use the yeast in a recipe (B), which could ruin the food if the yeast is no longer active. Instead, regular yeast can be tested or "proofed" by adding 2¼ tsp. or 1 envelope of yeast to ¼ cup of warm water, stirring, and waiting 10 minutes. If the yeast foams to double the water measure or ½ cup, it is still active. "Quick-rising" yeast, however, cannot be proofed this way (C); its fast-rising effect is lost by dissolving it in liquid.

72. A: Experts find that the majority of women tend to wear a small proportion of all the clothes they buy, from less than half to 20% or less. Few women wear over half of the clothes they buy (C), and fewer still wear most of them (B). It is also less accurate to say that women vary that much in

how many of the clothes they buy that they actually wear (D), because the most common pattern among women is to buy far more clothes then they end up wearing.

73. D: The most efficient way to sort clothes in the closet for finding them easily is first to sort them by category; e.g., pants all together, shirts all together; for women, skirts all together and dresses all together, etc. After sorting clothing categories, within each category they should then be sorted by color. It is not as easy to find individual items and assemble outfits by sorting into colors first and categories second (A). Putting favorite items most within reach (B) sounds like a good idea if we wear these the most, but is not as efficient as (D). Simply putting things wherever they can most easily be fitted in the closet (C) may be quicker and easier when putting clothes away, but will take longer and be harder to find things when getting dressed.

74. B: The "winter" palette is composed of cool colors and black and white for neutrals, which flatter the cool, blue-based skin tones of a "winter." Warm, yellow-based earth tones (A) are most flattering for the "autumn" palette of people with warm, yellow-based and olive skin tones. Light, soft pastels (C) are most flattering to the pale, delicate skin tones of "summer" people. Individuals with higher coloring are most flattered by the bright, vibrant colors (D) of the "spring" palette.

75. A: A medium-weight fabric, with just enough stiffness to skim over the body rather than cling to it (but not so stiff as to look boxy), with a flat texture that does not make body parts look bigger, is generally most flattering to overweight body types. Soft, fine-gauge knits (B) have a nice cuddly feel, but they cling to the body, showing off every lump and bump, so they are not as flattering to the overweight. Knits of larger gauge yarn with nubby textures (C) make a large body look even larger. Smooth, very shiny fabrics like silk or silky-looking synthetics (D) reflect the light, again making big bodies look bigger; and they may also be clingy.

76. A: Denim, as we commonly see in blue jeans, is made using a twill weave rather than a plain weave. Plain-weave fabrics are made by weaving one yarn over the other and then under it. Twill-weave fabrics are made by weaving the weft yarn under and then over two or more warp yarns at regular intervals. This creates a diagonal "twill line" or wale. Muslin (B), percale (C), and burlap (D) are woven using the plain weave, which is the least expensive and simplest way to weave fabrics.

77. B: In textile manufacturing, any knitted or woven fabric that just came off the loom and has not yet been finished is called "gray goods." This includes all fabrics that have not been singed, bleached (C); optically brightened, mercerized, dyed (A); printed, glazed, napped, stonewashed or tumbled; distressed; treated with anti-staining or anti-wrinkling finishes, etc. It does not refer only to gray-colored textiles (D).

78. B: According to symbols developed by the American Society for Testing and Materials (ASTM) and FTC, and adopted and disseminated by the American Cleaning Institute, a circle is the fabric care symbol meaning to dry clean a garment. A triangle (A) indicates a garment can be bleached. A square (C) means to dry the garment, with various added symbols indicating how to dry (e.g., line or hang dry, drip dry, dry flat, dry in shade, etc.). A circle inside of a square (D) indicates tumble drying, on any heat if the circle is clear. If the circle is black, it means tumble dry with no heat. A circle with one dot means low heat; two dots mean medium heat; and three dots mean high heat. Each of these symbols with an "X" over them means respectively NOT to dry clean, bleach, dry, or tumble dry.

79. C: The first step realtors recommend is for future home buyers to determine if they are ready to buy a home by identifying what they will need and want; e.g., whether buying is required or optional; whether they have a schedule for home buying; whether they are relocating; whether their lifestyle is changing, etc. The next step is to know whether potential buyers have the money for a down payment, closing costs, and monthly mortgage payments (A). The third step is to assure their credit is good enough to get a loan with the best terms (B): all debts (car notes, revolving credit card bills, lines of credit, monthly rent payments, etc.) are paid on time and otherwise as agreed. Realtors advise doing this for at least a year before buying a home. (Despite this time frame, maintaining or establishing good credit is not the first step realtors recommend.) Therefore, (D) is incorrect.

80. C: The realtor should regularly update information s/he gives the consumer about the conditions of the current housing market (A), available financing options (B), and situation-specific negotiating tactics (D). Buying a house can be a lengthy process, and market conditions can change, sometimes in relatively short periods. So can financing options: lenders can offer new products; different providers may offer different financing plans, and the realtor can recommend some that may suit the consumer better than others; the buyer's credit score and financial resources can change, etc. Also, some strategies for negotiating can apply to some situations, but not others wherein different techniques are more appropriate.

81. D: The primary consideration in real estate financing for home buyers is to find a mortgage loan that offers them the best terms (B) and costs them the least money (C) rather than simply being able to obtain a mortgage loan (A) at all, because almost anybody who is able and willing to pay high enough interest rates can obtain a mortgage. However, higher interest rates mean more of the consumer's money will go to interest rather than principal, requiring higher monthly payments that do not further reduce the principal balance owed for the property and taking longer to pay off the loan.

82. C: According to REALTOR.com, some home buyers prefer to look at listings of homes based on their locations (A); some want to look at listings based on their prices (D); some look at listings based on both their location and pricing criteria; some would rather have a local realtor suggest properties to them according to criteria they have communicated to the realtor (B); and many consumers like to combine these methods to maximize the number of potential properties they can consider. Which approach(es) they choose to look for a home is really up to the consumer.

83. A: In general, mortgage lenders require an outside third-party guarantee when the home buyer pays less than 20% of a house's list price as a down payment. Thus, they would definitely require such a guarantee if the down payment were less than 10% (B), but between 10% and 20% would still not be enough to waive this requirement. They do not require as much as 50% (C) down, which would more than double the millions of guaranteed mortgages generated annually. Lenders do not usually require 30% (D) down to waive the guarantee either.

84. B: Flood insurance not only covers the loss of or damage to a home due to flooding; it also covers the loss or damage of personal property and other contents within the home. Title insurance (A) only protects home buyers up to the real estate's mortgage value ("lenders" policies), and protects homeowners up to the purchase price of the home including down payments ("owners" policies) if the title to the real property turns out to be invalid. It does not cover personal property. Home warranties (C) cover workmanship in a new home, usually for the first year; wiring, plumbing, and other mechanical issues for the first two years; and structural defects in the building

for up to ten years. They do not cover personal property in the home. Therefore, it is incorrect that homeowners' insurance is the only form of insurance to cover personal property (D).

85. B: Housing meets human social needs most by providing a communal space where the essential unit of society, the family, can live. By providing a sense of privacy and personal space (A), housing meets human psychological needs. By providing shelter from the weather and giving people security (C), housing meets human physical needs. Since each of these represents a different type of human need, (D) is incorrect.

86. A: The traffic patterns in the floor plan of a house, i.e., how people move through it, are what most make the floor plan work well. Expert home builders say that successful floor plans are not determined by how they look to people when they are standing up (C) or sitting down (D), i.e., when they are still; but rather by how easily they navigate the home when they are moving. Some builders design homes where people go through one room to get to another rather than going through hallways (B), because they find this design makes it easier to see throughout the house and gives the effect of larger rooms.

87. A: In a family home, the parents are afforded more privacy if their master bedroom is not too close to a playroom or other parts of the house that tend to be noisy. To enhance togetherness with family members and guests, open floor plans often have kitchens, family rooms (B), and dining rooms (C) flowing together easily to facilitate visiting and preparing and serving meals. While parents and teenagers may like their bedrooms a bit farther apart for privacy, parents want their master bedroom closer to younger children's bedrooms (D) so they can more easily hear, see, check on, and get to them.

88. C: A design innovation in home construction is including some rooms planned to be flexible in purposes and use. This allows homes to change along with families. For example, when a grown child moves out, that child's bedroom can easily be converted to a home gym, home theater, craft room, etc. As children grow older, a playroom can become a game room, homework/studying room, hobby room, etc. This eliminates having to move to another house (A), which takes more money, time, and effort; and many families love their homes, neighbors, and neighborhoods and do not want to move. Remodeling (B) also costs more, and ongoing work inconveniences home living. While some "empty nest" parents may want to downsize to an apartment (D), this again involves more effort and time, even if proceeds from a house sale cover moving expenses. And some parents want to keep the space in their house for grown children, their families, and others to visit.

89. C: In 1899, eleven people convened a conference in Lake Placid, New York, to form a new discipline originally called home economics, later renamed family and consumer sciences. After a total of ten Lake Placid Conferences, a national organization originally called the American Home Economics Association (AHEA) was formed in 1909 (A). This organization's charter was enacted in 1910 (B). The AHEA adopted the Betty Lamp as its emblem in 1926 (D).

90. D: Ellen H. Richards was the first woman who graduated from Massachusetts Institute of Technology (MIT) and first female professor teaching there. She was an activist, for not only consumer education, but also women's rights, child protection, public health, nutrition, career education, industrial safety, keeping our air, water, and food pure, and applying principles of management and science to families. She formalized the family and consumer sciences profession and founded the AAFCS (originally American Home Economics Association/AHEA). Mildred Chamberlain (A) created the original design of the colonial Betty Lamp the AHEA adopted as its official symbol. Elizabeth C. Stanton (B) and Susan B. Anthony (C) were pioneers of the women's

rights and civil rights movements. (Interestingly, their work began in upstate New York, including Seneca Lake and Rochester; the AHEA was founded nearby in Lake Placid, three years after Anthony's death. Ellen Richards died just five years after Anthony. This area was home to many social reform movements during the late 19th and early 20th centuries.)

91. C: In most American high schools, taking Family and Consumer Sciences (formerly called Home Economics) will satisfy credits in Humanities, not Sciences (B), toward graduation. In most U.S. states, a Family and Consumer Sciences course is required in middle schools rather than being an elective (D). In most U.S. states, it is an elective course for high school students rather than a required course (A).

92. D: The ultimate and overall goal of FCS professionals is to help people make informed decisions that will improve their quality of life. They work toward this goal in numerous ways, including by applying their skills in communication, math, science, etc., to everyday living (A); by being educators (B), as well as being researchers, consultants, lobbyists, etc.; by evaluating and helping to improve consumer goods and services (C); and performing many other functions.

93. A: Both sisters were involved in promoting the domestic sciences prior to the birth of the home economics movement with the first of the Lake Placid Conferences in 1899. Catherine Beecher (B) was an educator, and her sister Harriet Beecher Stowe (C), an abolitionist known for authoring *Uncle Tom's Cabin.* They were both champions of women's education and early leaders in the foundations of home economics/family and consumer sciences. Therefore, that neither of them did this (D) is incorrect.

94. B: Gender stereotypes are attitudes, but often do attain legal status (A) when laws support them. For example, stereotypes of women as caregivers can prevent women from working outside home: Ireland's Constitution states its government should prevent mothers from having to "neglect" their household duties by assuring "economic necessity" does not require their outside "labour." While this law has good intentions to protect mothers from having to be both home managers and breadwinners, it can also limit mothers wanting to work outside the home from doing so. Thus even laws with good intentions can also do harm (C). Stereotypes influencing laws often discriminate against women, but not only women (D). For example, the president of South Africa pardoned women with children under 12 years who were convicted of nonviolent crimes from prison sentences in 1997. A single father also with a child under age 12 and convicted of a nonviolent crime petitioned to declare this women's pardon unconstitutional based on sex discrimination, but the Court judged it nondiscriminatory.

95. D: "Domesticity" equates to the labor-intensive nature of 19th-century households, whereas "modernity" equates to the labor-efficient nature of 20th- and 21st-century households. Historically, home economists focused on research into child development (A) and nutrition (B), and on furthering civil rights and equal rights movements (C) as parts of social reform. However, (D) is the only activity area that both took place around the turn of the centuries and also effected the transition from the domestic household to the modern one.

96. C: Occupational family and consumer sciences courses are mainly for teaching students how to prepare themselves to seek and obtain paying employment, not necessarily for establishing lifelong careers (B). They are not for teaching students how to manage being homeowners (A), or for teaching them how to balance their future family and work lives (D). The focus of occupational FCS programs is to learn and apply FCS skills, knowledge, and attitudes that will help them secure paid jobs.

97. A: Analyzing how career decisions can affect family and work balance is Competency 1.1.4 of Standard 1.0, Career, Community, and Family Connections. The comprehensive standard for this area is "Integrate multiple life roles and responsibilities in family, work, and community settings." Consumer and Family Resources (B) is Standard 2.0; its comprehensive standard is "Evaluate management practices related to the human, economic, and environmental resources." Family and Community Services (C) is Standard 7.0; its comprehensive standard is "Synthesize knowledge, skills, and practices required for careers in family and community services." Consumer Services (D) is Standard 3.0; its comprehensive standard is "Integrate knowledge, skills, and practices needed for a career in consumer services."

98. B: "Analyze energy efficient methods" is Competency 5.2.6 under Content Standard 5.2. "Demonstrate a waste minimization plan" (A) is Competency 5.4.2 under Content Standard 5.4, "Apply hazardous materials and waste management procedures." "Design energy efficient methods" (C) is Competency 5.4.6, also under Content Standard 5.4 (see above). "Apply security procedures" (D) is Competency 5.5.2 under Content Standard 5.5, "Demonstrate a work environment that provides safety and security.

99. C: "Demonstrate standard procedures for receiving and storage of raw and prepared foods" is Competency 9.2.6 under Content Standard 9.2, "Apply risk management procedures to food safety, food testing, and sanitation." "Apply principles of food production to maximize nutrient retention in prepared foods" (A) is Competency 9.3.3 under Content Standard 9.3, "Evaluate nutrition principles, food plans, preparation techniques and specialized dietary plans." "Design instruction on nutrition for health maintenance and disease prevention" (B) is Competency 9.4.5 under Content Standard 9.4, "Apply basic concepts of nutrition and nutritional therapy in a variety of settings." "Establish par levels for the purchase of supplies based on an organization's needs"   (D) is Competency 9.6.8 of Content Standard 9.6, "Demonstrate food science, dietetics, and nutrition management principles and practices."

100. C: "Demonstrate measuring, estimating, ordering, purchasing, pricing, and repurposing skills" is Competency 11.3.3 of Content Standard 11.3. "Critique design plans to address client's needs, goals, and resources" (A) is Competency 11.6.4 of Content Standard 11.6: "Evaluate client's needs, goals, and resources in creating design plans for housing and residential and commercial interiors." "Describe features of furnishings that are characteristic of various historical periods" (B) is Competency 11.5.1 of Content Standard 11.5: "Analyze design and development of architecture, interiors, and furnishings through the ages." "Demonstrate procedures for reporting and handling accidents, safety, and security incidents" (D) is Competency 11.8.4 of Content Standard 11.8: "Analyze professional practices, procedures for business profitability and career success, and the role of ethics in the housing, interiors and furnishings industries."

101. B: This competency is Competency 13.6.3 of Content Standard 13.6, "Demonstrate standards that guide behavior in interpersonal relationships." Under Content Standard 13.5, "Demonstrate teamwork and leadership skills in the family, workplace, and community" (A), an example of one competency is Competency 13.5.5: "Demonstrate ways to organize and delegate responsibilities." Under Content Standard 13.3, "Demonstrate communication skills that contribute to positive relationships" (C), an example of one competency is Competency 13.3.1: "Analyze communication styles and their effects on relationships." Under Content Standard 13.4, "Evaluate effective conflict prevention and management techniques" (D), an example of one competency is Competency 13.4.3: "Apply the roles of decision making and problem solving in reducing and managing conflict."

102. B: The competency quoted is Competency 15.2.2 of Content Standard 15.2, "Evaluate parenting practices that maximize human growth and development." Under Content Standard 15.4, "Analyze physical and emotional factors related to beginning the parenting process" (A), an example of one competency is Competency 15.4.3: "Analyze implications of alternatives to biological parenthood." Under Content Standard 15.3, "Evaluate external support systems that provide services for parents" (C), an example of one competency is Competency 15.3.1: "Assess community resources and services available to families." Under Content Standard 15.1, "Analyze roles and responsibilities of parenting" (D), an example of one competency is Competency 15.1.5: "Explain cultural differences in roles and responsibilities of parenting."

103. D: In the laboratory method of learning, students do not listen to lectures or take notes. Rather, they participate directly in hands-on observations and experiments. These direct experiences often stimulate students' interest and motivation (A) for a subject more than reading textbooks or listening to lectures alone can. The laboratory method also affords students the chance to participate in original research (B), which can be very exciting and can earn them credit and recognition for research in the field of the course they are studying. Moreover, in this method students learn skills for using the instruments and equipment (C) in the lab, a valuable asset for future lab courses, internships, and employment.

104. B: The steps in the demonstration method of instruction are in this sequence: First, the teacher introduces the topic or problem and what will be demonstrated (C). Second, the instructor demonstrates the process that s/he is teaching; this is the development (D). Third, the instructor completes the process being demonstrated, and class and teacher draw conclusions about it (A). Fourth, the teacher guides the students in evaluating (B) what was demonstrated and what they have discovered and learned from it; and/or the teacher evaluates what the students have learned by testing the knowledge they should have gained through observing the demonstration.

105. B: Four components of the communication process are encoding (A), wherein the sender converts information into symbols representing the ideas involved; the medium (D) whereby the sender transmits the message, e.g., visual, oral, or written; decoding (C), whereby the receiver(s) will interpret the message received in terms of the receiver(s)'s own experiences to gain meaning from the symbols sent (and correct interpretation equals successful communication); and feedback (B), whereby the receiver(s) responds to the sender's message. Feedback includes the receiver's saying something in return, including asking a question; making a facial expression or gesture; writing a message; taking some physical action; or not saying or doing anything. As in this example, even silence is a type of response. In this case, the fact that the receivers did not laugh (or groan, as at a bad pun) indicates that either they did not think the joke was funny or they did not understand it.

106. C: The principle of leading honestly and ethically in the Leadership Process Model includes actively building trust with team members by keeping one's word and supporting member needs; communicating and acting authentically; consistently doing the right thing; and showing integrity and humility. The principle of focusing on relationship development (A) in this model includes developing one's emotional intelligence, which involves self-awareness, emotional self-regulation, and acting consistently with one's ethical values; showing empathy for team members; and rewarding team members for their work. The principle of being aware of actions and reactions (B) includes being a good role model; controlling one's emotions in the workplace; and keeping in mind the employee and business consequences of what one says and does. The principle of consciously assigning tasks (D) includes matching specific tasks to individual team members' greatest skill strengths and particular situations.

107. C: The FCCLA's mission to promote students' personal growth and development through Family and Consumer Sciences education aims to help them develop life skills focused on their roles in society as earners of wages (A), members of families (B), and leaders in their communities (D). Although some wage earners, family members, and community leaders are certainly also business owners (C), this is not one of the main roles that the FCCLA specifically focuses on in helping students develop their skills for living.

108. B: According to the AAFCS, its certification in Education Fundamentals can help recipients obtain employment and continuing education in both corporate businesses and nonprofits; in both public and private schools (A); in elementary, middle, secondary, and post-secondary or higher education (C); and in both schools and after-school programs (D).

109. C: In recent years some researchers studying how FCS teachers adopt technology in their instruction (e.g., cf. Redmann and Kotrlik, LSU) have investigated related variables, such as the teachers' ages (A); the availability of technology (B); teachers' technology anxiety (C); and barriers to integrating technology (D) like technology-to-student ratio, effective software for their courses, technical support, sufficient time to schedule technology use, and administrative support. Of these, teachers' anxiety about technology seems to have more impact on the variability of teachers' technology adoption than the others.

110. C: These are all true. Historically, curricular deficits developed out of the original separation of academic courses from vocational courses (A), and the parallel separation of students bound for college from students not bound for college (B). Since the implementation of the Common Core Standards, many states now integrate literacy in all vocational and technical subjects with literacy in all academic subjects (D) like language arts, math, science, and social studies.

111. B: One basic principle of effective classroom management is that it should teach the students to manage their own behaviors, rather than teachers' always having to manage them. Though classroom management techniques are necessary to address disruptive behaviors when they do happen, they should also focus on reducing nondisruptive behaviors that are nevertheless off-task (A). Students who are off-task are not engaged in learning. Students are not simply taken off-task by external distractions (C); it is more normal and natural for them to be off-task than on-task (D). Therefore, classroom management is necessary for students to learn to be engaged in learning activities and stay on-task.

112. C: The food and appliance industry currently is seeing increases in the number of jobs available for FCS professionals. The rapidity of social change today increases individual stress throughout the life span; this increases the need for human services administration rather than reducing it (A). Health care jobs, especially long-term care administration, wellness, and dependent care, are not remaining stable (B) but are increasing. Employment opportunities in the hospitality industries, i.e., hotels, motels, and restaurants, and travel and tourism industries are not currently decreasing (D), but expanding as well.

113. A: Within the wide range of specialties available in FCS education, financial planning is one that is currently needed by many financial institutions. This includes brokerage firms; banks and savings and loan associations, which *are* also looking for financial planners (B); and insurance companies and also counseling agencies (C). Qualified financial planners *do* need to understand both the relationship with community and also family dynamics (D) to serve these financial institutions best.

114. A: FCS graduates who choose careers in marketing consumer products and services may provide personal counseling in nutrition, parenting, financial management, and eldercare as well as doing or managing direct sales promotion, providing customer service in resorts, restaurants, hotels, and tourism or convention centers, or monitoring consumer trends, needs, and satisfaction. Conducting market surveys (B) is one job description among careers in research for FCS graduates. Improving product or service design in laboratories (C) is one job description among careers in product and service development for FCS graduates. Implementing plans for marketing consumer goods or services (D) is one job description among careers in operations management for FCS graduates.

115. D: One learning activity that is useful for students to develop career goals is for teachers to ask them to make a list of activities giving them the most feelings of accomplishment, satisfaction, and enjoyment; and then select one favorite. Then teachers can have them explain why they like each activity and think of occupations fitting with the preferences and interests they have identified. Considering what they are good at doing is not enough; there are some things people have abilities or talents for, but do not necessarily prefer or enjoy (A). Although being practical is good, students should not just pursue the most available jobs if they involve activities they do not enjoy (B): they will not like these jobs, making it difficult for them to perform well at them and/or stay in them. For students with no job experience, it is better to identify their interests first and then match these to occupations, rather than try to select preferences among occupations (C).

116. D: When students are learning how to participate successfully in job interviews, they should learn to come prepared for standard interview questions, even though they may not be asked all of these in every interview (D). Coming to job interviews without this preparation makes applicants appear uninformed, inexperienced, immature, or even silly. Interview posture should be appropriate rather than extreme; for example, leaning forward slightly indicates interest in what the interviewer is saying, but sitting rigidly on the edge of the chair or slouching in the seat are equally poor choices (A). Applicants should NOT chew gum during an interview, and even if an interviewer invites them to smoke, they should NOT (B). Most workplaces today are smoke-free. Applicants should not initially ask interviewers what a job's salary and benefits are (C). This makes them seem interested only in these things and not in the work the job involves. Applicants should only discuss pay and benefits when or if the interviewer brings them up.

117. D: In job interviews, conversations, and other interactions at work, school, and social situations, good body language includes using one's hands when talking in a confident, relaxed way that is natural for the individual. Playing with one's hair or biting one's nails does not appear natural (A); it makes one appear nervous, insecure, bored, or inattentive and is also impolite. Clasping the hands together or clenching them in fists (B) is also bad body language; forcing oneself not to move the hands at all is not normal. Large, broad, sweeping hand movements (C) are also not the best way to express oneself in interview, work, school, or social situations as these are exaggerated and overly dramatic rather than appropriate.

118. B: This reflects the AAFCS Code of Ethics' Core Value: "Support life-long learning and diverse scholarship." Other Core Values include: "Believe in the family as a fundamental unit of society"; thus (A) is incorrect; "Seek new ideas and initiatives and embrace change"; hence (C) is incorrect; and "Promote an integrative and holistic approach, aligned with the FCS body of knowledge, to support professionals who work with individuals, families, and communities"; hence (D) is incorrect.

119. A: The AAFCS Code of Ethics' Statement of Principles of Professional Practice includes under the heading of Integrity that its members "avoid practices that harm, exploit, or intimidate others" and "endeavor to maintain the credibility of the profession by demonstrating integrity." Under Confidentiality (B), principles include protecting the confidential information of persons in their professional relationships, and forming and sustaining trust, cooperation, respect, and confidentiality in professional relationships. Under Conflict of Interest (C), principles include members' actively avoiding conflicting roles and exploitation of people with whom they work; and being responsible for treating others fairly and preventing, in fact or in appearance, divided loyalties. Under Professional Competence (D), principles include credentials, professional development, accurate representation and professional designation, competency claims, and practicing within the law and one's qualifications.

120. D: In the AAFCS Code of Ethics Statement of Principles of Professional Conduct, the principle of Integrity includes that "AAFCS members...avoid making misleading or inaccurate communications." The Conflict of Interest principle includes that "AAFCS members...avoid the fact or appearance of divided loyalties" (A). The Confidentiality principle includes that "AAFCS members maintain and guard the confidentiality of persons with whom they have professional relationships" (B). The Professional Competence principle includes that "AAFCS members practice within the law and within the recognized boundaries of their education, training, and experience" (C).

Practice Test #2

Practice Questions

1. Research has found which of the following most often?
   a. Parents are more likely to expect more of their youngest children.
   b. Parents are more likely to expect more from their middle children.
   c. Parents are more likely to expect the same from all their children.
   d. Parents are more likely to expect more of their firstborn children.

2. The child who assumes the role of the family artist, rebel, peacemaker, troublemaker, clown, or negotiator is most often which child in birth order?
   a. The firstborn child
   b. The middle child
   c. The second child
   d. The only child

3. The Family and Medical Leave Act of 1993 requires employers to give eligible employees unpaid time off with job protection. Which of these *most* accurately identifies the reasons allowed for this leave?
   a. Maternity leave exclusively.
   b. Maternity *or* paternity leave.
   c. Maternity *and* paternity leave.
   d. Family and/or medical reasons.

4. When children become part of a remarried family with other children, which of these is true?
   a. A child's rank in the family never changes.
   b. The role each child plays remains distinct.
   c. All these factors are most likely to change.
   d. Incest taboos are the same for all siblings.

5. According to Evelyn Duvall's description of the Family Life Cycle, which of these accurately represents two consecutive stages of the family life cycle?
   a. Married couples without children; families with children from birth to 6 years
   b. Families with children from birth to 6 years; families with children 6-13 years
   c. Families with children 0–30 months; families with children 24 months-6 years
   d. Families with teen children 13–20 years; "empty nest" couples to retirement

6. In some models of family life stages, which task is most typical of the "later family life" stage?
   a. Helping children develop peer relationships
   b. Assuming the care for one's family of origin
   c. Reminiscing and integrating life experiences
   d. Coping with deaths in one's family of origin

7. Which of these correctly relates a stage in each theory to the same age periods and family stages?

    a. Freud's Oedipal; Erikson's Autonomy vs. Shame, Doubt; Piaget's Preoperational; Duvall's School Age

    b. Freud's Anal; Erikson's Industry vs. Inferiority; Piaget's Formal Operations; Duvall's with Preschoolers

    c. Freud's Genital; Erikson's Initiative vs. Guilt; Piaget's Concrete Operations; Duvall's with Teenagers

    d. Freud's Oral; Erikson's Basic Trust vs. Mistrust; Piaget's Sensorimotor; Duvall's Families with Infants

8. Freud's Latency stage corresponds most closely in terms of child development with

    a. Kohlberg's Pre-Conventional stage in his theory of moral development.

    b. Erikson's psychosocial development stage, Identity vs. Role Confusion.

    c. Piaget's stage of cognitive development he termed Formal Operations.

    d. Duvall's Families with School-Age Children stage of family development.

9. Erikson's psychosocial developmental stage of Ego Integrity vs. Despair corresponds to which of Duvall's stages of family development?

    a. Stage VIII: Aging Families

    b. Stage VII: Middle-Aged Families

    c. Stage VI: Families as Launching Centers

    d. Stage IV: Families with School-Age Children

10. According to the attachment styles defined by Mary Ainsworth through her Strange Situation experiments, which of these did she observe about separation anxiety in children aged 12–18 months?

    a. Children who have secure attachments show distress when their mothers leave the room.

    b. Children with insecure-ambivalent attachment show no distress if mother leaves the room.

    c. Children with insecure-avoidant attachment show extreme distress at the mother's leaving.

    d. Children with secure attachment show higher separation anxiety than insecure-ambivalent.

11. According to Diana Baumrind's theory of parenting styles, which style is considered the ideal?

    a. Permissive

    b. Authoritarian

    c. Authoritative

    d. Uninvolved

12. Baumrind and other researchers applying her theory of parenting styles have found that children who function at low levels in multiple areas of life are most likely to have had parents with which style?

    a. Permissive

    b. Authoritarian

    c. Uninvolved

    d. Authoritative

13. According to Schaefer's model of parenting along continua across two dimensions, which of these most accurately corresponds with Baumrind's subsequent definition of parenting styles?

    a. Parents high in warmth/low in hostility and high in control/low in autonomy have a permissive style.

    b. Parents high in hostility/low in warmth and high in autonomy/low in control have authoritarian style.

    a. Parents high in autonomy/low in control and high in hostility/low in warmth have an uninvolved style.

    d. Parents high in warmth/low in hostility and high in autonomy/low in control have authoritative style.

14. According to Bandura's Social Learning Theory, four conditions are needed for modeling of behaviors to occur. Which of these is most related to having a good reason to imitate another's behavior?

    a. Attention

    b. Motivation

    c. Retention

    d. Reproduction

15. Which of the following more accurately reflects what Bandura believed in developing his social learning theory?

    a. The environment an individual is in causes his or her behavior.

    b. Environment, behavior, and psychological processes interact.

    c. The behavior of an individual creates his or her environment.

    d. Psychological processes cause the environment and behavior.

16. Regarding needs parents must meet for children, which of the following is correct according to the hierarchy of needs Abraham Maslow proposed in his humanistic theory of motivation and personality?

    a. Parents must make children feel they are loved before worrying about their feeding and rest.

    b. Enabling children to fulfill their highest potentials in life takes precedence over all other needs.

    c. Before they can keep children safe, parents must see they get enough water, food, and sleep.

    d. Parents should promote children's self-esteem first and then their family acceptance and love.

17. When a couple with children divorces, which family relationship factors often receive direct and/or indirect effects?

    a. The structure of the family

    b. The income for the family

    c. Community expectations

    d. All these can be affected

18. A variety of researchers have found evidence that family recreation provides many benefits, both to families and to individual family members. Which of the following is an example of one of family recreation's benefits to the family as a group?

    a. Teaching moral values and health

    b. Improvements in communications

    c. Providing educational experiences

    d. Fulfilling a diversity among needs

19. In which of Erikson's stages of development do individuals measure their success by what they contribute to their families and society?
    a. Intimacy vs. Isolation
    b. Ego Integrity vs. Despair
    c. Identity vs. Role Confusion
    d. Generativity vs. Stagnation

20. In describing stages of child development, which ages did Arnold Gesell characterize as periods of equilibrium, consolidation, and smoothness?
    a. 2½, 5½ to 6, and 11 years
    b. 2, 5, 10, and 16 years
    c. 3½, 7, and 13 years
    d. 4, 8, and 14 years

21. In the developmental tasks he identified for different age groups across the life span, which of the following did Robert Havighurst include as a task during middle age?
    a. Adopting civic responsibilities
    b. Adjusting to physical changes
    c. Meeting social/civic obligation
    d. Socially responsible behaviors

22. When describing moral development, Piaget characterized two types of adult-child relationships. In the _____ relationship, the adult _____ the child; in the _____ relation, the adult _____ the child.
    a. Heteronomous, "co-operates" with; autonomous, coerces
    b. Unilateral, respects; reciprocal, controls and/or constrains
    c. Interactive, constrains; heteronomous, "co-operates" with
    d. Heteronomous, coerces; autonomous, "co-operates" with

23. According to psychologists, the level of Safety needs in Maslow's hierarchy would typically be a priority for which developmental period?
    a. Infancy
    b. Adulthood
    c. Adolescence
    d. Toddlerhood

24. A child whose developmental tasks include learning to play in groups, to identify as a female or male, and to have a basic understanding of right and wrong is typically in which life stage?
    a. The toddler years
    b. Early school years
    c. Middle school age
    d. Birth to two years

25. During which life stage is it most typical to focus on developmental tasks like thinking abstractly, attaining peer group membership, and experiencing sexual relationships?
    a. Early adolescence
    b. Later adolescence
    c. Middle school age
    d. In early adulthood

26. According to models of developmental tasks at various life stages, when is an adult most likely to develop a perspective related to death?
    a. Around age 22–34
    b. Around age 34–60
    c. Around age 60–75
    d. Around 75–death

27. Which special needs are most often characteristic in autism spectrum disorders?
    a. Difficulty focusing and maintaining attention
    b. Difficulty understanding and using social cues
    c. Difficulty with motor control and coordination
    d. Difficulty with adhering to consistent routines

28. Which special resource(s) would most likely be needed by someone with spina bifida?
    a. A communication board
    b. Text-to-speech software
    c. A wheelchair or crutches
    d. Cochlear implantation(s)

29. The impact on a child's development of local and global communities belongs in which of the systems in Bronfenbrenner's ecological systems theory?
    a. The chronosystem
    b. The microsystem
    c. The mesosystem
    d. The exosystem

30. Whereas Freud focused on male development in proposing the concept of the Oedipal conflict, neo-Freudians expanded on his theory to include the Elektra conflict for girls. In the latter, what must a girl do to resolve this conflict and thereafter have successful interpersonal relationships?
    a. Nothing; they just grow out of it
    b. Symbolically "kill" their mothers
    c. Want to be just like their fathers
    d. Want to be just like the mothers

31. The research of Walter Toman (also adopted by Murray Bowen) found that in the workplace, which relationship is likely to be most harmonious and effective?
    a. A boss and an assistant who were both oldest children working together
    b. A boss and assistant who were both youngest children working together
    c. A boss who was an oldest child and an assistant who was a youngest child
    d. A boss who was a youngest child and an assistant who was an oldest child

32. Family therapist Virginia Satir identified five common roles of family members. She described only Levelers, who communicate their true feelings honestly, as healthy because their outward communication is congruent with their inward emotions. Which of the other four dysfunctional roles hopes to be loved by being perceived as harmlessly endearing?
    a. Blamers
    b. Placators
    c. Distractors
    d. Computers

33. In describing high-context vs. low-context styles of communication, what do "sender-oriented values" mean?
    a. The speakers do not consider the values of the listeners.
    b. The speaker has responsibility for clearly communicating.
    c. The speaker lets listeners be responsible to understand.
    d. The speaker uses indirect patterns of verbal orientation.

34. Which of the following is true about one channel of nonverbal communication?
    a. Eye contact while speaking is one culturally dependent orientation.
    b. Eye contact while speaking is treated universally across all cultures.
    c. Eye contact while speaking is preferred in Japan as long and direct.
    d. Eye contact while speaking is direct for all USA audience members.

35. Regarding nonverbal forms of communicating, which statement is most accurate?
    a. Messages conveyed via nonverbal means are not found as truthful as verbal messages are.
    b. The use of humor in speaking is not included among the areas of nonverbal communication.
    c. Increasing globalization means that nonverbal communication is more universally the same.
    d. Increasing globalization requires more awareness, observation, and sensitivity of speakers.

36. When giving advice, which example is the recipient most likely to hear instead of perceiving it as unsolicited, unwanted, and coercive?
    a. "You may find that easier to do if you try doing this."
    b. "You must do it this way or it's never going to work."
    c. "There is only one way to do that right and this is it."
    d. "That's not working because you're doing it wrong."

37. Among the following developmental theories, what is correct relative to development across the life span?
    a. Freud and Piaget had theories that cover the life span, while Erikson's ends at adolescence.
    b. Piaget's and Erikson's theories do not go beyond adolescence while Freud's goes to death.
    c. Freud's and Erikson's theories cover all of life while Piaget's theory stops with adolescence.
    d. Erikson's theory has developmental stages across the life span; Freud's and Piaget's do not.

38. Among the following, which is an example of a consumer right?
    a. Minimizing environmental impacts through purchasing choices
    b. Following safety instructions to ensure the safe use of products
    c. Sustainable consumption that will not impinge on others' needs
    d. Accessing information that supports better purchasing decisions

39. Which provision of the Wall Street Reform and Consumer Protection Act of 2009 fulfills the consumer rights and responsibilities regarding redress?
    a. Brokers have advisors' duties if advising on investments.
    b. Advisors must give information to the SEC upon request.
    c. Whistleblowers who disclose wrongdoing are protected.
    d. Consumers can sue credit rating agencies for negligence.

40. When was the Federal Trade Commission (FTC) established?
    a. 1914
    b. 1934
    c. 1979
    d. 1995

41. One factor that influences consumers to consider prices more in their health care decisions is:
    a. When they have no prior ideas of provider quality.
    b. When their health insurance plan is a PPO or HMO.
    c. When they have a severe and/or urgent condition.
    d. When they have health care practitioners they like.

42. When using product or service information to inform consumer decisions, which of these is an example of "soft" information?
    a. Weight
    b. Pricing
    c. Quality
    d. Content

43. In determining one's current financial situation for financial planning, what is true about which elements to include?
    a. For planning purposes, use total income after taxes.
    b. Living expenses and debts are really the same thing.
    c. When listing assets, including savings is unnecessary.
    d. When listing income, use gross income before taxes.

44. Which of these is most realistic about analyzing financial values and developing financial goals?
    a. Other people cannot recommend any financial goals for an individual.
    b. Other people should advise an individual of goals and which to pursue.
    c. Individuals must decide for themselves which financial goals to pursue.
    d. Financial goals should include saving and investing but never spending.

45. What is true about information on clothing labels, tags, or packages?
    a. Manufacturers are required by law to provide only registered ID number identification.
    b. Manufacturers are required by law to show ID, fiber content, country, and care instructions.
    c. Manufacturers are required by law to indicate only the country where clothing is made.
    d. Manufacturers are required by law to show fiber content; care instructions are optional.

46. What information is required by law for Nutrition Facts panels on food packaging to include?
    a. Serving size, number of servings, and calories per serving
    b. Amounts of protein, carbohydrates, and fats per serving
    c. Fiber, sodium, vitamins, and minerals are not necessary.
    d. All of these and more information are required by law.

47. In the Nutrition Facts panels on food packages, how is the amount of calcium represented?
    a. The number of milligrams
    b. In number of micrograms
    c. As percent of serving size
    d. As percent of Daily Value

48. Among the following cognitive biases to which management is subject, which one is caused by making a decision based on an incorrect generalization from an isolated instance or a sample that is too small?
    a. Prior hypothesis bias
    b. Illusion of control bias
    c. Representativeness bias
    d. Escalating commitment bias

49. As two separate ways of improving decision-making in management, what is a major difference between devil's advocacy and dialectic inquiry?
    a. Alternative reassessments
    b. The number of alternatives
    c. Acceptance of alternatives
    d. Effects of greater diversity

50. Relative to prioritization for time management, what does the "80/20 Rule" mean?
    a. 80% of the people in any workplace contribute 20% of the effort.
    b. 80% of what we do contributes less than 20% to our work's value.
    c. The formula for work success is 80% perspiration, 20% inspiration.
    d. In typical workplaces, 80% of time is well used and 20% is wasted.

51. In researching elder-care services online, which website helps consumers find their local Area Agency on Aging (AAA)?
    a. Medicare website: http://medicare.gov/
    b. LeadingAge (IAHSA) website: http://www.leadingage.org/
    c. Eldercare.gov website: http://eldercare.gov/
    d. Assisted Living Federation website: http://www.alfa.org/alfa/

52. When working parents look for services to care for their children, which of these is accurate?
    a. Because of recent economic factors, many caregivers are charging higher rates.
    b. Grandparent child care is less common with fewer extended families cohabiting.
    c. To be competitive, "hybrid" providers offer parents additional services included.
    d. Au pairs' wages are a bigger challenge than associated government regulations.

53. Which of the following websites is *best* for finding energy-efficient home appliances at no charge?
    a. www.sears.com/
    b. http://products.construction.com/
    c. www.consumerreports.org
    d. www.energystar.gov

54. Safety is a primary consideration in choosing toys for children. Experts also advise choosing toys from which children can learn; that keep their attention more than briefly; that do not promote aggression; and that parents will also enjoy playing with and will not find irritating. What else is recommended in choosing toys?
    a. Parents should choose different toys for girls than toys they pick for boys.
    b. Social interaction and creativity are equally important for toys to promote.
    c. Toys that stimulate one sense at a time rather than several are preferable.
    d. Problem-solving supersedes eye-hand coordination in what toys develop.

55. The nutritional requirements of women:
    a. Differ from the requirements of men.
    b. Are accurately described by all these.
    c. Vary throughout the menstrual cycle.
    d. Differ when pregnant and/or nursing.

56. Which of these is most accurate about nutritional needs among African-American people?
    a. They are more likely to have certain conditions due to cultural dietary choices.
    b. Their nutritional requirements are no different than those of other Americans.
    c. Their genetic predisposition to certain conditions influences nutritional needs.
    d. They develop certain conditions because they cannot afford nutritious foods.

57. Vegetarians can get non-heme iron from plant sources, but to improve absorption of these, they should eat them together with foods rich in:
    a. Calcium.
    b. Vitamin C.
    c. Vitamin D.
    d. Vitamin E.

58. Which of these dairy foods has the most calcium?
    a. A 4.2-oz. slice of fruit cheesecake
    b. A 5.3-oz. serving of low-fat yogurt
    c. A 1.4-oz. chunk of cheddar cheese
    d. A 2.6-oz. serving of plain ice cream

59. Which of these vitamins build up to harmful levels in the body if too much are ingested?
    a. Vitamins C and D
    b. Vitamins A, D, E, K
    c. Vitamin B complex
    d. Vitamins never do

60. The USDA recommends that in a healthy diet, at least half of the plate should be:
    a. Proteins, with grains.
    b. Vegetables and dairy.
    c. Grains and dairy food.
    d. Fruits and vegetables.

61. Which of these is true about the %DV (Daily Value) the FDA requires on food labels?
    a. They make it easier for consumers to know in numbers how much they need of nutrients in a day.
    b. They make it easier for consumers to know how much of a day's allowance of nutrients a food has.
    c. They make it harder for consumers to comparison shop for foods by the relative nutrient amounts.
    d. They were developed by the FDA to replace RDAs because the RDAs were found to be inaccurate.

62. Which of the following disorders *always* involves bingeing and purging by definition?
   a. Neither one
   b. Anorexia
   c. Bulimia
   d. Both

63. Which is *most* accurate today about type 1 and type 2 diabetes?
   a. Type 1 diabetes is only inherited, while type 2 diabetes only develops from lifestyle.
   b. Type 1 diabetes is from lack of insulin; type 2 diabetes is from insensitivity to insulin.
   c. Type 1 diabetes occurs in childhood, while type 2 diabetes occurs during adulthood.
   d. Type 1 diabetes accounts for half of all cases and type 2 diabetes for the other half.

64. Which of the following is most consistent with expert advice for healthy eating?
   a. Tracking eating patterns causes obsession and compulsion.
   b. Exercising is a superior antidote for boredom than eating is.
   c. An effective way to decrease food intake is skipping meals.
   d. Certain foods that are not healthful should never be eaten.

65. When used for weight management, which component of cognitive-behavioral therapy (CBT) is most reflected in a person's not eating in certain environments?
   a. Positive self-statements
   b. Readiness for change
   c. Breaking linkages
   d. Self-monitoring

66. When planning a menu, which should be decided upon first?
   a. What the entrée of the meal will be
   b. What side dishes of the meal will be
   c. What the décor for the meal will be
   d. What to prepare with foods bought

67. Which of these reflects proper dining etiquette when attending dinner parties?
   a. When passing dishes, they should be passed clockwise.
   b. Bread only should be passed around the table clockwise.
   c. Guests should pass all dishes including bread to the right.
   d. It is up to the individual guests whether to cut up foods.

68. Among these food preparation factors, which can cause food poisoning or other food-borne illness?
   a. All of these can cause it with certain foods.
   b. Cooking foods for the wrong lengths of time
   c. Cooking foods at the wrong temperatures
   d. Not pasteurizing or refrigerating some foods

69. Which of these cooking methods is the most energy-efficient?
   a. A microwave oven
   b. A convection oven
   c. An electric oven
   d. A gas oven

70. Of the following types of fat, which is considered the *most* harmful?
    a. Partially hydrogenated vegetable oil
    b. Fully hydrogenated vegetable oil
    c. Monounsaturated fat
    d. Polyunsaturated fat

71. Which of the following is *most* accurate regarding freeze-dried cheese?
    a. Freeze-dried cheese costs more than fresh cheese does.
    b. Freeze-dried cheese is less expensive than fresh cheese.
    c. Experts advise replacing fresh cheeses with freeze-dried.
    d. No reconstituting method makes it just like fresh cheese.

72. What do wardrobe experts advise to women for cleaning out their closets?
    a. To get rid of anything they have not worn in more than a year
    b. To get rid of anything that does not fit them and keep the rest
    c. To get rid of anything and everything meeting all these criteria
    d. To get rid of anything that is not suited to their personal styles

73. When reorganizing clothes, which is the best advice regarding clothing colors?
    a. We should discard any items in colors outside of our most flattering color group.
    b. We should keep a few items in colors outside our color group to ensure variety.
    c. We should coordinate all the colors of our clothes for maximum outfit potential.
    d. We should do (A) and (C) to look our best and make creating outfits the easiest.

74. Some color analysts divide people's coloring into the four seasons for choosing the most flattering palette of colors in clothing and makeup. Others use adjectives associated with temperaments for the same purpose. Which of the following correctly equates these two systems?
    a. "Passionate" = "Autumn"; "Dramatic" = "Winter"; "Vibrant" = "Spring"; "Romantic" = "Summer"
    b. "Dramatic" = "Autumn"; "Passionate" = "Winter"; "Romantic" = "Spring"; "Vibrant" = "Summer"
    c. "Vibrant" = "Autumn"; "Romantic" = "Winter"; "Passionate" = "Spring"; "Dramatic" = "Summer"
    d. "Romantic" = "Autumn"; "Vibrant" = "Winter"; "Dramatic" = "Spring"; "Passionate" = "Summer"

75. Of the following, which would be the most flattering cut and line to wear for a woman with large hips and thin legs?
    a. A circle skirt
    b. A pencil skirt
    c. A fishtail skirt
    d. An A-line skirt

76. In fabric that is woven using a triaxial weave, what is the third set of yarn called?
    a. The warp
    b. The weft
    c. The whug
    d. The woof

77. In the process of finishing knitted or woven fabrics, which of these reflects the correct sequence?
    a. Bleaching or brightening, cleaning, dyeing, singeing, Mercerizing
    b. Cleaning, singeing, bleaching or brightening, Mercerizing, dyeing
    c. Mercerizing, bleaching or brightening, dyeing, cleaning, singeing
    d. Bleaching or brightening, dyeing, Mercerizing, singeing, cleaning

78. Which of the following fabric care symbols indicates a garment should be line-dried or hang-dried?
    a. A square with diagonal lines in a corner
    b. A square with one horizontal line inside
    c. A square with three vertical lines inside
    d. A square with a horizontal arc at the top

79. Which of the following is true about purchasing a home, according to realtors?
    a. To buy a house with a mortgage, some down payment is always necessary.
    b. When purchasing a home, the buyer is always responsible for closing costs.
    c. Some loan programs give buyers no money down and few/no closing costs.
    d. Monthly mortgage payments are not affected by the down payment made.

80. Which of these is most accurate about realtors who help consumers buy homes?
    a. Some realtors represent buyers, while others represent sellers.
    b. All practicing realtors represent both the buyers and the sellers.
    c. Some realtors represent buyers or sellers, while others do both.
    d. Whether realtors represent buyers or sellers varies individually.

81. Why do realtors usually advise consumers to obtain pre-approval before choosing a home to buy?
    a. To determine how much money they can afford to spend
    b. To be able to accomplish all of these through pre-approval
    c. To identify which loan programs will meet their needs best
    d. To allow time to find lenders and have their credit checked

82. In the realty market, in most U.S. states a "first-time buyer" means:
    a. Anyone who has never owned real estate property before.
    b. Anyone who has only owned property less than six months.
    c. Anyone who has not owned property in the last three years.
    d. Anyone who did own, but does not currently own, property.

83. Where can a consumer obtain a mortgage loan to buy a house?
    a. Consumers can acquire loans from any and all of these sources today.
    b. Mortgage bankers or mortgage brokers are the only sources for loans.
    c. Savings and loans, credit unions, various banks, or insurance companies
    d. Increasing numbers of realtors can arrange mortgage financing today.

84. When should a home buyer get warranty and insurance coverage for the home?
    a. After closing before moving in
    b. When making a bid on a house
    c. At the closing of the home sale
    d. When applying for a mortgage

85. Regarding the essential human right to housing, which of the following UN events took place the earliest in history?
    a. The United Nations appointed its first Special Rapporteur on Adequate Housing.
    b. The United Nations held its first Conference on Human Settlements, or Habitat I.
    c. The United Nations declared the International Year of Shelter for the Homeless.
    d. The United Nations' Universal Declaration of Human Rights, including to housing.

86. Some home construction companies design houses based on certain principles. Which of the following is a general rule reflecting good design principles?
    a. There should be only one way to get to the kitchen.
    b. It is better to have several ways to get to any room.
    c. Traffic patterns going through rooms disrupt activity.
    d. Separate rooms look bigger than in open floor plans.

87. In the interior design of a family home, what is true about the placement of windows?
    a. Windows can give good views but no practical benefits.
    b. Windows have a tendency to make homes look smaller.
    c. Windows are good regardless of number and positions.
    d. Windows can create relationships with nature outdoors.

88. When a home construction company advertises new homes as "energy-efficient" or "energy-saving," which of these are the houses most likely to be?
    a. Houses built using building principles and techniques that are more energy-efficient
    b. Houses built in the traditional/standard way but fitted with energy-saving appliances
    c. Houses built to minimize impacts on the environment, regardless of costs or comfort
    d. Houses built to reduce energy used by electronics, which consume the most energy

89. What is the Betty Lamp?
    a. A modern lighting innovation
    b. A colonial lighting appliance
    c. It was (B) and is also now (D)
    d. The symbol of the AAFCS

90. The AAFCS supports the FCS profession. What is true about its leadership?
    a. It works to enhance the well-being of individuals, families, and communities.
    b. It influences consumer use of goods and services but not their development.
    c. It has a vision and mission to shape social change but not specific public policy.
    d. It works to supply leadership to consumers and professionals in all these areas.

91. Which of the following is a division of the AAFCS?
    a. The National Association of Teachers of Family and Consumer Sciences (NATFACS)
    b. None of these is a division of the American Association of Family and Consumer Sciences.
    c. The National Association of Teacher Educators of Family and Consumer Sciences (NATEFACS)
    d. The National Association of State Administrators of Family and Consumer Sciences (NASAFACS)

92. As a historical basis relative to gender stereotypes, which of these have been most instrumental in getting women the rights to vote, run for office, inherit and own property, obtain citizenship for their children, and other equal human rights?
   a. State institutions
   b. Individual women
   c. Women's movements
   d. (B) and (C) more than (A)

93. How did the Morrill Act (1862) further the domestic sciences in America?
   a. By funding industrial colleges with a land grant to teach household management to farm wives
   b. By funding industrial colleges with a land grant to teach farm husbands agricultural techniques
   c. By funding states with equal land grants for founding agricultural colleges, like with the Turner Plan
   d. By funding enforcement of a law banning bigamy and limiting church/nonprofit land ownership

94. How has the United Nations been involved in studying and dispelling worldwide gender stereotypes?
   a. The United Nations has not been directly involved with addressing gender stereotypes.
   b. Through such groups and actions as an entity for gender equality and panel discussions
   c. Only through advisory and technical services that further role models and best practices
   d. It has undertaken to examine the impacts of gender stereotypes but not address them.

95. A high school family and consumer sciences class is learning skills to use in job interviews. The teacher asks the students what questions they might ask the interviewer. What student's question would be appropriate?
   a. "Will I be able to change my schedule if I'm hired?"
   b. "What kind of work is it that your company does?"
   c. "Now that we have had an interview, am I hired?"
   d. "When would you want me to start if I am hired?"

96. In household management, which of the following would be the first step to take in the process of solving a problem?
   a. To identify alternatives among actions
   b. To predict outcomes of various actions
   c. To collect data concerning the problem
   d. To identify what the problem actually is

97. The competency, "Apply a variety of assessment methods to observe and interpret children's growth and development" is found under which of the National Standards for Family and Consumer Sciences?
   a. Family
   b. Human Development
   c. Education and Early Childhood
   d. Family and Community Services

98. In the National Standards for Family and Consumer Sciences, under Area of study 8.0, Food Production and Services, which of the following is a competency under Content Standard 8.2, "Demonstrate food safety and sanitation procedures"?
    a. "Demonstrate safe and environmentally responsible waste disposal and recycling methods."
    b. "Demonstrate professional skills in safe handling of knives, tools, and equipment."
    c. "Demonstrate procedures for safe and secure storage of equipment and foods."
    d. "Use computer based menu systems to develop and modify menus."

99. Area of Study 10.0, Hospitality, Tourism, and Recreation of the Family and Consumer Sciences National Standards includes Content Standard 10.2: "Demonstrate procedures applied to safety, security, and environmental issues." Which of the following is a competency under this Content Standard?
    a. "Apply industry standards for service methods that meet expectations of guests or customers."
    b. "Examine lodging, tourism, and recreation customs of various regions and countries."
    c. "Apply facility management, maintenance, and service skills to lodging operations."
    d. "Demonstrate procedures for assuring guest or customer safety."

100. Area of Study 12.01 of the Family and Consumer Sciences National Standards is Human Development. In this area, Content Standard 12.1 is: "Analyze principles of human growth and development across the life span." Which of the following Human Development Competencies falls under this Content Standard?
    a. "Analyze the effect of heredity and environment on human growth and development."
    b. "Analyze the effects of gender, ethnicity, and culture on individual development."
    c. "Analyze physical, emotional, social, spiritual, and intellectual development."
    d. "Analyze the role of communication on human growth and development."

101. Nutrition and Wellness, which is Area of Study 14.0 of the National Standards for Family and Consumer Sciences Education, includes this competency: "Explain physical, emotional, social, psychological, and spiritual components of individual and family wellness." Under which of the following Content Standards does this competency belong?
    a. 14.2: "Evaluate the nutritional needs of individuals and families in relation to health and wellness across the life span."
    b. 14.5: "Evaluate the influence of science and technology on food composition, safety, and other issues."
    c. 14.1: "Analyze factors that influence nutrition and wellness practices across the life span."
    d. 14.4: "Evaluate factors that affect food safety from production through consumption."

102. The National Standards for Family and Consumer Sciences Education includes Textiles, Fashion, and Apparel as Area of Study 16.0. In this area, one competency is: "Explain the ways in which fabric, texture, pattern, and finish can affect visual appearance." This competency is found under which of these Content Standards?
    a. 16.2: "Evaluate fiber and textile products and materials."
    b. 16.3: "Demonstrate fashion, apparel, and textile design skills."
    c. 16.4: "Demonstrate skills needed to produce, alter, or repair fashion, apparel, and textile products."
    d. 16.7: "Demonstrate general operational procedures required for business profitability and career success."

103. Which of the following is a disadvantage of the laboratory method of learning?
    a. The laboratory method uses experience so students learn by doing.
    b. The laboratory method enhances learning with multisensory modes.
    c. The laboratory method involves more time and expense in learning.
    d. The laboratory method gives students preparation directly for living.

104. Of the following, which is an advantage of the demonstration method of teaching?
    a. Students can become more passive and dependent.
    b. Students can learn best when the classes are smaller.
    c. Students can develop observation skills and curiosity.
    d. Students can learn but the method takes much time.

105. Business experts find the most important element of total quality management to be effective communication. Which of the following is true about business communication?
    a. A company can maintain high quality without good communication.
    b. Poor communication leads to interpersonal mistrust in a company.
    c. Communication quality has no effect on productivity in a company.
    d. Poor communication causes misunderstandings rather than anger.

106. According to some business experts, five kinds of thinking processes are needed for strategic leadership. A leader discerns patterns or connections among abstract ideas and assembles these to create a full picture. This description defines which type of thinking?
    a. Intuitive thinking
    b. Innovative thinking
    c. Conceptual thinking
    d. Implementation thinking

107. The FCCLA (Family, Career and Community Leaders of America) student organization helps its members to develop personally through Family and Consumer Sciences education and several areas, e.g., character development and creativity. Among four other areas, which is reflected in a student's evaluating several different insurance policies on multiple features and selecting the most suitable one?
    a. Career preparation
    b. Critical thinking skill
    c. Practical knowledge
    d. Interpersonal communication

108. Of the following career information that young people need, which is most likely to help them identify their career interests and preferences?
    a. Exposure to higher education and other lifelong learning opportunities
    b. Exposure to information on job opportunities that lead to living wages
    c. Training in job-seeking skills and in basic workplace skills ("soft skills")
    d. Participating in career assessments and job-based exploration activity

109. Which of the following most accurately represents the relationship between FCS educators and Special Education for students with special needs?
    a. FCS educators can offer Special Education teachers strategies for teaching life skills.
    b. FCS educators' educational preparation typically excludes alternative assessments.
    c. FCS educators always need Special Ed. teacher advice on differentiated instruction.
    d. FCS educators need Special Ed. teachers for team-teaching special-needs students.

110. Of the following AAFCS resolutions related to public legislation, which is the most recent?
  a. Life & Career Choices Class Requirement
  b. The resolution about Basic Health Literacy
  c. The resolution regarding Healthy Weight
  d. 10th anniversary of UN Year of the Family

111. The National Association of Teacher Educators for Family and Consumer Sciences assigned work groups to examine requirements of National Standard 9, Student and Program Assessment, of the National Standards for Teachers of Family and Consumer Sciences. In 2005 these work groups reported four expectations for beginning or pre-service FCS teachers. Which choice accurately reflects one of these expectations?
  a. They should know, but not interpret, standards and criteria for FCS programs and student learning.
  b. They should collect data about programs and learning using only normed, standardized assessment.
  c. They should both reflect and refer to external evidence, but not thereby change teaching practices.
  d. They should justify decisions for program design and teaching practices using data-based evidence.

112. For students preparing for careers in FCS, where do food manufacturers have jobs open?
  a. Only in product development and marketing
  b. Consumer affairs, public policy, and research
  c. They need FCS graduates in all of these areas.
  d. They have no jobs open in strategic planning.

113. What are some important skills that FCS graduates specializing in fashion design and interior design need to have for working on design teams or operating, managing, and/or owning private design businesses?
  a. Their technical knowledge is more important than their creative abilities.
  b. They need business expertise, as well as all skills named in these choices.
  c. Having global awareness is more important than expertise with business.
  d. Creative abilities are imperative whereas other skills are not as important.

114. Which of these is correct regarding what students must do to qualify for a career in FCS?
  a. The minimum degree required for employment in the field of FCS is the master's degree.
  b. Students must participate in internship programs during 4-year, but not 2-year programs.
  c. Additional education courses and practice teaching are required for teaching certification.
  d. Graduate work is needed to teach college, do research, or supervise, but not other jobs.

115. What is most accurate about what students should learn about completing job applications?
  a. If information is already on résumés they prepared, they need not write it on application forms.
  b. They should include all education and experience rather than tailor applications for certain jobs.
  c. Details like handwriting, spelling, and following directions matter less than making an impression.
  d. They should never lie on job applications, but keeping unfavorable information brief is advised.

116. Which of the following best represents good advice to job applicants for successful interviews?
    a. It is good to back up statements about oneself with specific examples.
    b. Direct eye contact with interviewers is intimidating and to be avoided.
    c. Be prepared to answer interviewer questions but not to ask questions.
    d. If one does not understand a question, do not let on and seem foolish.

117. Of the following, which is generally a good practice for writing a résumé?
    a. Students with no work history should place education first on a résumé.
    b. Education or work history should start with the earliest and go forward.
    c. As employers may request personal references, put them in a résumé.
    d. In work histories, it is best to include reasons for leaving previous jobs.

118. The AAFCS Code of Ethics holds members responsible for actively avoiding exploiting people with whom they work or interact professionally. In which category of professional practice does the AAFCS place this principle?
    a. Professional Competence
    b. Respect for Diversity
    c. Conflict of Interest
    d. Confidentiality

119. The AAFCS expects its members to adhere to its professional conduct principle of Integrity. Which of the following reflects this principle?
    a. Protecting private information
    b. Making ethically sound decisions
    c. Practicing within expertise limits
    d. Treating consumers with fairness

120. According to the AAFCS Code of Ethics Statement of Principles of Professional Practice, AAFCS members do not claim to have expertise in areas wherein they are not educated, trained, and experienced. To which of the following principle categories does this relate?
    a. Integrity and Confidentiality
    b. Professional Competence
    c. Respect for Diversity
    d. Conflict of Interest

Answers and Explanations

1. D: Research studies have consistently found that parents are more likely to expect more from their firstborn children. New parents with no previous experience of having their own children are likely to place higher expectations on their first child. By the time they have had more children and experience, they are likely to lower their expectations of their middle (B) and youngest (A) children to be more realistic. Hence most parents are not likely to have the same expectations of all their children (C).

2. C: Researchers have observed that a family's second-born child may take on one of the roles named. A second child often feels s/he gets less attention than the first child and resents being compared to the older sibling. Some rebel against feeling bossed around by the older sibling as well as the parents. Firstborn children (A) are more likely to take on roles of "little parents" by being responsible, conservative, and high-achieving. Middle children (B) tend to play very independent roles and feel relief at less pressure from parents; but also experience less attention, appreciation, and family involvement. Only children (D) may interact better with adults than other children, but are not known to assume the roles named as often as second children are.

3. D: The Family and Medical Leave Act of 1993 requires employers to give qualified employees up to 12 weeks of unpaid leave with their jobs, salaries, and benefits protected for certain medical and family reasons. The law does not specify that this is for maternity leave only (A); or for a choice of either maternity or paternity leave but not both (B); or for both maternity and paternity leave but not for other reasons (C). An employee might take long-term disability leave under this law for an extended illness, and many companies also apply the available duration of long-term disability for maternity and/or paternity leave. Historically, employers gave this leave to new mothers since the law was enacted; and in recent years, companies have increasingly been offering paternity leave to new fathers as well.

4. C: When adults remarry and their respective children are blended into one family, a child's family rank often changes (A); e.g., a child who was formerly the eldest may now be the second or third oldest child, and is treated as such by the rest of family. The roles played by each child also often become less clear (B) than they were in their previous family's dynamics. Additionally, because stepsiblings have no blood relation, incest taboos among them are also less clear-cut (D) than among biological siblings.

5. C: Duvall's Stages of the Family Life Cycle are: (1) childless married couples; (2) families with children 0–30 months; (3) families with children 24 months to 6 years; (4) families with children 6–13 years; (5) families with children 13–20 years; (6) families launching children, from the first child gone to the last child leaving home; (7) middle-age parents, from "empty nest" to retirement; and (8) aging family members, from retirement to both spouses' deaths. The second stage in (A) incorrectly ends with 6 years instead of 30 months. The first stage in (B) incorrectly represents Stage 2 as ending at 6 years instead of 30 months, and the second stage named in (B) represents Stage 4, skipping Stage 3; thus these two are not consecutive. The two stages in (D) are also not consecutive: they name Stages 5, families with teenagers; and Stage 7, middle-age couples from "empty nest" to retirement, skipping Stage 6, families launching children.

6. C: The "later family life" stage is the last stage of some models (cf. Carter & McGoldrick, 1999; Carr, 2006), when family tasks include coping with physical deterioration in oneself and others and with losing spouses and peers; parents' relinquishing, and adult children's assuming, more responsibility to maintain families; and elder members' reminiscing, reviewing their lives,

integrating their life experiences, and preparing for death. Helping children develop relationships with their peers (A) is a typical task of the "family with young children" stage. Assuming care for one's family of origin (B) is typically a task during the "family with adolescents" stage. Coping with deaths in one's family of origin (D) is typically a task involved in the stage of "launching children."

7. D: Freud's Oral stage corresponds to infancy, as does Erikson's stage of Basic Trust vs. Mistrust, Piaget's Sensorimotor stage, and Duvall's Families with Infants stage. Freud's Oedipal stage (A) corresponds to preschool; Erikson's corresponding stage is Initiative vs. Guilt, rather than toddlerhood's Autonomy vs. Shame and Doubt; Piaget's Preoperational stage corresponds to preschool, but Duvall's corresponding stage is Families with Preschoolers, not School Age. Freud's Anal (B) stage corresponds to toddlerhood; Erikson's corresponding stage is Autonomy vs. Shame and Doubt, not Industry vs. Inferiority, which occurs during elementary/middle school ages. Piaget's stages corresponding to toddlerhood are the end of the sensorimotor and beginning of the preoperational, not formal operations, which develops around adolescence. Toddlerhood falls between Duvall's Families with Infants and Families with Preschoolers stages. Freud's Genital (C) stage is in adolescence, as is Duvall's Families with Teenagers, but Erikson's corresponding stage is Identity vs. Role Confusion, not infancy's Basic Trust vs. Mistrust; Piaget's is Formal Operations, not the elementary/middle school years' Concrete Operations.

8. D: Freud's Latency stage of psychosexual development corresponds with the elementary and middle school years; therefore, Duvall's family development stage of Families with School-Age Children corresponds most closely to it. Kohlberg's Pre-Conventional stage of moral development (A) corresponds to the preschool years; Freud's corresponding stage is the Oedipal. Erikson's psychosocial stage of Identify vs. Role Confusion (B) and Piaget's Formal Operations stage of cognitive development (C) both correspond to adolescence; Freud's corresponding stage is the Genital.

9. A: Erikson described people undergoing his stage of Ego Integrity vs. Despair in their old age, which corresponds to Duvall's eighth and last stage of Aging Families. Both feature adapting to the process of aging, conducting a life review, and preparing for death as tasks in common for adults. Duvall's Stages VII, Middle-Aged Families (B) and VI, Families as Launching Centers (C), correspond to Erikson's stage of Generativity vs. Stagnation. These share common tasks for adults of leaving legacies to children and grandchildren. Duvall's stage IV, Families with School-Age Children (D), corresponds most to Erikson's stage of Industry vs. Inferiority; both share common tasks for children of meeting new social and academic demands.

10. A: Ainsworth found in her experiments that children with secure attachments to their mothers showed distress when their mothers left the room. She expanded the work of John Bowlby, who defined separation anxiety as a characteristic of normal attachment. Ainsworth found that children she identified as having insecure-ambivalent attachment showed more extreme distress at their mothers leaving than securely attached children, rather than showing no distress (B). However, she found that children she defined with insecure-avoidant attachment showed no distress upon their mothers' leaving the room, rather than showing extreme distress (C). Therefore, children with secure attachment show normal separation anxiety, but this is a lower level of separation anxiety than the level displayed by children with insecure-ambivalent attachment, not higher (D).

11. C: According to Baumrind, the authoritative parenting style is ideal in its combination of high standards, clear expectations, reasoned discipline, and warmth and nurturance. Authoritative parents give children balanced amounts of independence and guidance, respect and love, and firmness and kindness. The permissive (A) parenting style is very loving and warm, but also overly

indulgent and lacking in limits, consequences, and control. The authoritarian (B) parenting style is overly controlling and rigid while lacking in warmth. The uninvolved (D) parenting style lacks both warmth and control.

12. C: Baumrind and others after her who have applied her theory in research have found that children who function at low levels in multiple life areas are likely to have had parents with the uninvolved parenting style. This style makes few demands of children, but also demonstrates little warmth toward them. The children thus lack both parental discipline and parental nurturing. Extremes of the uninvolved parenting style include rejecting and/or neglecting children. As a result, children perform poorly and are likely to be depressed and engage in delinquent behaviors. Children with permissive (A) parents are likely to be impulsive, seem immature, lack self-control, and avoid responsibility. Children with authoritarian (B) parents are likely to behave well, but also to lack initiative, avoid leadership roles, and are moody. Children with authoritative (D) parents are likely to be well-behaved but also independent; self-reliant, socially responsible, achievement-oriented, and to have high self-esteem.

13. C: Schaefer's dimensions are (1) along a continuum from warmth to hostility, and concurrently (2) along a continuum from autonomy to control. Comparing these to Baumrind's parenting styles, low control and low warmth equates to her Uninvolved style. Parents with Baumrind's Permissive style (A) have Schaefer's high warmth, but also high autonomy, not low. Parents with Baumrind's Authoritarian style (B) have Schaefer's high hostility, but also high control, not low. Parents with Baumrind's Authoritative style (D) have a balance of Schaefer's dimensions: enough but not excessive (i.e., intrusive, codependent) warmth; sufficient control to set reasonable limits and enforce rules consistently, but not so much to be rigid or overly punitive; enough autonomy to let children make their own decisions and learn from their mistakes, but not so much to leave children without the structure and guidance they need. While high warmth with high control (A) in Schaefer's model does not correlate with a Baumrind parenting style, this combination is often characterized as "smother love."

14. B: Bandura said that in order for modeling of behaviors to be effective, the four conditions of attention, retention, reproduction, and motivation were necessary. Attention (A) requires the observational learner to attend to the behavior modeled. Degrees of attention are affected by multiple variables like the functional value of the behavior, its complexity, distinctiveness, prevalence, and affective valence (how emotionally attractive the observer finds it), and the observer's level of arousal, sensory capacities, perceptual set, and having received past reinforcement for similar behaviors and/or for observing others' behaviors. Motivation (B) is most related to the observers' having good reason(s) for observing and imitating others' behaviors, e.g., previous rewards, imagined or promised rewards, and vicarious; i.e., observing others being rewarded for behaviors. Retention (C) involves being able to remember the behaviors one observed. Reproduction (D) involves imitating or replicating the observed behavior.

15. B: Traditional behaviorists believed that an individual's environment caused the individual's behaviors (A). Bandura proposed that not only do the individual's behaviors also cause the environment (C), which he *reciprocal determinism;* i.e., the environment and the behaviors mutually determine one another, but moreover that the individual's psychological processes (D) also interact with environment and behavior to produce learning and shape the personality. Thus he did not believe that any one of these factors caused any other(s), but that all three reciprocally interact and influence each other.

16. C: In his theory, Maslow proposed a progressive hierarchy of needs, often illustrated in a pyramid: He proposed each level of needs must be met before any higher level(s). The most basic needs essential to survival, which must be met first, are at the pyramid's base/bottom. Maslow termed these physiological needs, e.g., food, water, and sleep. As these come before all others, (A) is incorrect. At the pyramid's point/tip/top, Maslow placed "self-actualizing needs," i.e., to fulfill one's highest potentials. These can only be realized after all other needs lower on the pyramid are met; hence (B) is incorrect. Maslow placed "security needs," i.e., for shelter and safety, second after physiological needs (C). Needing to feel love, affection, and belonging, i.e., what Maslow called "social needs" are third in his hierarchy; what he termed "esteem needs," i.e., to have self-esteem and feel personal worth, social recognition, and accomplishment are fourth. Hence (D) is incorrect.

17. D: When parents divorce, the family structure is necessarily changed; this is the most direct and obvious effect. However, it is very common for divorce also to change the family's income (B): One parent may have custody of all children but half the income of the couple or less; when couples split custody among several children, the parents' two households may have unequal incomes; divorce court-ordered child support and alimony may be less or more than the previous income of the couple; some parents fail to pay the ordered child support, etc. Community expectations (C) are also often affected: divorce can change where family members live, their types of homes, and where the children attend school; this in turn can cause neighborhood pressures on a family. All of these factors can change the family dynamics.

18. B: One of many benefits of family recreation researchers have found is that it improves communication within the family. Teaching moral values and healthy lifestyles (A) is a benefit researchers have found family recreation provides children as individual members of the family; providing children with educational experiences (C) is another. Fulfilling the diverse needs (D) of different family members is more of a challenge to planning and engaging in family recreation that researchers have found, rather than a benefit of family recreation to either the family group or individual family members. (Of course meeting the needs of all family members would be a benefit of family recreation when this is actually accomplished; however, researchers have not identified it as a benefit but a challenge, because it is so difficult to achieve with no existing universal structure for programming family recreation.)

19. D: Erikson's stage of Generativity vs. Stagnation occurs in middle adulthood, when people focus on creating legacies to leave for future generations, such as children, businesses, homes, inventions, and other contributions to family and society. Those who stagnate rather than generate become self-absorbed. Intimacy vs. Isolation (A) occurs in young adulthood, when people either succeed at forming intimate relationships with others or become isolated from them. Ego Integrity vs. Despair (B) occurs during old age, when people review their lives and feel either satisfaction or regret. Identity vs. Role Confusion (C) occurs during adolescence, when teens either succeed at establishing a personal identity or become confused about what their role is.

20. B: Gesell characterized the ages of 2 years, 5 years, 10 years, and 16 years as times when children's development is marked by balance (equilibrium), consolidation of abilities, and emotional smoothness or stability. He described the ages of 2½, 5½ to 6, and 11 years (A) as times when children's previous patterns are breaking up, resulting in disequilibrium and more difficult behaviors. Gesell characterized the ages of 3½, 7, and 13 years (C) as times when children are internalizing and integrating things: 3½-year-olds show unbalanced physical coordination and emotional insecurity, while 7-year-olds and 13-year-olds tend to rebel and/or withdraw. He described the ages of 4, 8, and 14 years (D) as periods when children's development is marked by "vigorous, expansive" movement toward the outside world.

21. B: Havighurst included in developmental tasks he defined of middle age (35 to 60 years) the need to adjust to the physiological changes that occur with aging. He included adopting civic responsibilities (A) as a developmental task of early adulthood (18 to 35 years). He included meeting social and civic obligations (C) as a developmental task of later life (60 years and older). He included developing socially responsible behaviors (D) as a developmental task of pre-adolescence and adolescence (12 to 18 years).

22. D: Piaget named a unilateral (B) or one-sided morality and adult-child relationship, based on obedience to authority, heteronomous or controlled by others. He named an independently constructed morality, and an adult-child relationship of reciprocal respect, as autonomous. The adult coerces the child in the heteronomous relation and "co-operates" (i.e., collaborates in performing operations) with the child in the autonomous one, rather than vice versa (A). The autonomous relation involves interaction and cooperation whereas the heteronomous involves adult constraint of the child rather than the opposite (C).

23. D: In infancy (A), Maslow's first level of Physiological needs takes priority. In adulthood (B), people may give priority to any or several of his needs levels depending on their circumstances. However, assuming they have met all the other levels, adults are most likely to be concerned with the highest level of self-actualization needs. In adolescence (C), the third and fourth levels of need, for love and belonging and for esteem, are likely to have priority. Whereas infants are most concerned with meeting their needs to sleep, be fed, changed, etc., in toddlerhood the emphasis typically progresses to meeting their needs for safety and security.

24. B: Children in the early school years, e.g., from four to six years old, have developmental tasks including learning to play in groups, identifying with a gender role, and early moral development. Toddlers (A), e.g., from two to four years old, have developmental tasks including locomotion beyond toddling; symbolic representation and pretend play; developing language; and learning self-control. Children in middle school (C), e.g., from six to twelve years old, have developmental tasks including making friends; performing concrete mental operations; learning academic and social skills; participating as a team member in playing games; and evaluating themselves. Infants (A), e.g., from birth to two years old, have developmental tasks including motor, perceptual, and sensory maturation; basic emotional development; social attachment; sensorimotor cognition; understanding basic causation, objects, and categorizing.

25. A: The developmental tasks named are characteristic of early adolescence, around the ages of 12 to 18 years old. Typical developmental tasks in later adolescence (B) include establishing one's sex role identity, becoming independent of one's parents, developing an internalized moral sense, and making career choices. Typical developmental tasks at middle school age (C), around six to 12 years old, include forming and maintaining friendships; performing concrete mental operations; learning academic and social skills; self-evaluation; and engaging in team play. Typical developmental tasks in early adulthood (D) include starting to work at a job, getting married, and having children.

26. C: It is more typical for adults to develop a perspective regarding death in later adulthood than in old age when closer to death (D). By old age they usually have already established a point of view about death and are occupied with reviewing their lives, adjusting to the deaths of spouses, etc. Young adults (A) are typically engaged in other developmental tasks like marrying, starting families, and working. Middle-aged adults (B) are typically involved in tasks like developing their marriages, households, and careers and parenting their children.

27. B: A common characteristic in autism spectrum disorders is not understanding others' social cues, and hence also not using those cues to communicate socially. For example, an autistic individual might not understand that another person's smiling indicates happiness and/or friendliness, and may feel these emotions but not realize that smiling communicates them to others. Attentional deficits (A) are special needs more commonly associated with ADHD. Autistic people are more likely to focus intensely on one activity or subject for prolonged times. Motor control and coordination difficulties (C) are more common in developmental disabilities like cerebral palsy. (Autistic people may engage in odd-looking and/or repetitive movements, but this is not a motor difficulty.) Many autistic individuals adhere very rigidly to consistent routines rather than having difficulty with doing so (D); with autism, it is commonly a bigger problem if that routine is disrupted, which can cause "meltdowns"; or if someone wants to convince the autistic person to change a routine.

28. C: Certain types of spina bifida cause paralysis. The vertical location of the defect in spinal column closure dictates how high the paralysis occurs: in some patients the bladder and bowels are affected, while in others it may be limited to the feet and lower legs. A common symptom is inability or difficulty in walking. Communication boards (A) are for people who cannot speak for cognitive (e.g., intellectual disability) or neuromuscular (e.g., cerebral palsy) reasons or vocal system disorders. Text-to-speech software (B) is also for people who cannot speak normally, including those with autistic disorders, deafness, ALS, etc. Cochlear implantations (D) are to restore hearing for those with sensorineural hearing loss.

29. D: What Bronfenbrenner named the exosystem represents the wider social system, including such factors as local and global communities, community resources available to the child's family, the work schedules of the child's parents, etc., that affect the child's development. The chronosystem (A) is what Bronfenbrenner called the temporal system that affects the child's environment, including processes and events like the child's physiological maturation, cognitive development, or parental deaths, divorces, and other experiences that alter development and life. The microsystem (B) is Bronfenbrenner's term for the interactions and relationships a child has with people in the family, neighborhood, school, and other environments. The mesosystem (C) is what Bronfenbrenner called the connection between parts of the microsystem, such as between parents and teachers, etc. (Bronfenbrenner also identified the macrosystem, meaning the system of beliefs, values, laws, customs, and other cultural influences on the child.)

30. D: Freud theorized that young boys unconsciously desired their mothers and wanted to get rid of their fathers as competition for the mother's attentions. He called this the Oedipal conflict after the Greek character who unknowingly killed his father and married his mother. While Freud omitted girls from this concept, neo-Freudians following him expanded it to include the Elektra conflict. Just as Freud said boys resolved the Oedipal conflict by wanting to be just like and emulating their fathers (C), neo-Freudians said girls resolved the Elektra conflict by wanting to be just like their mothers and imitating them. This is called "identification with the aggressor" because the child unconsciously fears retaliation by the same-sex parent for his or her aggressive impulses. Neither Freud nor the neo-Freudian psychologists believed girls just grow out of (A) the conflict. Symbolically "killing" the mother (B) is not how girls resolve the conflict; it is rather the impulse to do so that they resolve by identifying with the mother.

31. C: Toman found in his research that an oldest child, who grew up being comfortable with a leadership role, will have a complementary relationship in the workplace with an assistant who grew up as a youngest child and is more comfortable with following the leader. (Youngest children

may also like being in charge, but usually have different leadership styles than oldest children.) A boss and assistant who both grew up with the same sibling positions {(A), (B)} are more likely to clash by being too similar in motivations and styles. A boss who was a youngest child and an assistant who was an oldest child (D) are less likely to have as effective a relationship, as their respective roles are more likely mismatched to their interactional personality characteristics. (Murray Bowen also incorporated Toman's findings into his Family Systems Theory, making it better known.)

32. C: Distractors are described by Satir as those members who divert the others' attention from problematic issues and the attendant emotions by engaging in various attention-getting behaviors. Distractors may be the "babies" of their families, and feel the others will only love them if perceiving them as harmless and cute. Blamers (A) hide their insecurities by attacking the others. Placators (B) try to appease the others to avoid the rejection or disapproval they fear. Computers (D) avoid confronting or expressing feelings by denying all emotion and limiting their communication to only intellectual, objective, or factual topics.

33. B: Sender-oriented values are characteristic of low-context communication, wherein the speaker is responsible for the clarity of his or her communication, rather than the listeners having responsibility for understanding it (C). This does not mean the speaker ignores the values of the listeners (A). In low-context communication, which has sender-oriented values rather than interpreter-sensitive values (where the listener is responsible to understand), the speaker uses direct patterns of verbal orientation rather than indirect patterns (D), which are used in high-context communication.

34. A: Like gestures and other nonverbal channels of communication, eye contact is a culturally dependent orientation. It is not viewed the same universally across all cultures (B). For example, in Japan, listeners prefer indirect eye contact with speakers and avoid prolonged or direct eye contact (C). Even in the USA, where direct eye contact is considered more important while speaking, public speakers are still advised to make direct eye contact with only some audience members but use indirect eye contact with others (D) according to their individual preferences. In America, knowing which audience members prefer direct or indirect eye contact is a skill required for public speaking.

35. D: While increasing globalization means that cultures are mixing and communicating more, this does not mean that nonverbal forms of communication have become more universally similar (C). It means rather that people are exposed to more culturally dissimilar forms of nonverbal communication, requiring speakers to become more aware, observant, and sensitive to these cultural differences. People generally assume nonverbal communication to be more truthful than verbal communication, not vice versa (A). Humor *is* classified among the major areas of nonverbal communication (B), as are areas like paralinguistics, proxemics, gestures, posture, body language, facial expressions, eye contact, etc.

36. A: This example suggests ("may," "if," "try") rather than insisting, as with "must" (B), "only one way to do that right" (C), or negating as in "doing it wrong" (D). Example (A) not only offers a mild suggestion, which the recipient is more likely to accept; it also frames the advice as being in the recipient's best interest. The other examples do not; instead, they give commands, implying that the speaker assumes power over the recipient. The recipient is more likely to reject or resist these as attempts at coercion. The form of communication in (A) is more likely to promote cooperation and prevent conflict; those in the other choices are more likely to promote defensiveness and/or conflict.

37. D: Erikson's theory of psychosocial development is the only one of the three named whose stages include young adulthood, middle adulthood, and old age until death. Freud's and Piaget's theories both have stages that end with adolescence. Freud's theory of psychosexual development ended with adolescence because he believed the personality was essentially formed by then. Piaget's theory of cognitive development ended at adolescence because he believed his highest stage of Formal Operations was attained by then. (Later researchers have found some adults never attain it.) Of the three, only Erikson included adult developmental stages in his theory.

38. D: Having access to information that supports better purchasing decisions is an example of the consumer's right to education. Minimizing environmental impacts through purchasing choices (A) is an example of a consumer's *responsibility* to promote a healthy environment. An example of the consumer's *right* to a healthy environment is to reside and work in environments that are not detrimental to the consumer's health. Following safety instruction to ensure the safe use of products (B) is an example of a consumer's *responsibility* for safety. An example of a consumer's *right* to safety is to be protected against health hazards in products and services. Sustainable consumption that will not impinge on others' needs (C) is an example of a consumer's *responsibility* to meet basic needs. An example of a consumer's *right* to have basic needs met is to have access to shelter, water, and food.

39. D: The provision of the Wall Street Reform and Consumer Protection Act of 2009 that consumers can sue credit rating agencies for negligence fulfills the consumer's right and responsibility concerning redress, i.e., to request compensation for an agency's wrongdoing. This law's provision that brokers have the same fiduciary duties as advisors if they give investment advice to consumers (A) fulfills the consumer's right to be given accurate product information, and the responsibility to analyze and apply that information judiciously; and the consumer's right to have access to education to inform purchasing decisions, and the responsibility to pursue consumer education about products as they change. The law's provision that advisors disclose information to the SEC on request (B) also fulfills the consumer's right and responsibility to information [see (A) above]. The law's provision of protection to whistleblowers (C) fulfills the consumer right and responsibility to be heard.

40. A: The FTC was established by the administration of President Woodrow Wilson in 1914 through the FTC Act and the Clayton Act as the anti-trust legislation of the New Freedom. 1934 (B) was when the Securities and Exchange Commission (SEC) was established under the administration of President Franklin D. Roosevelt to regulate the stock market and securities industry; the SEC took over enforcement of the Securities Act from the FTC, which originally enforced it before SEC formation. Three of five initial SEC commissioners came from the FTC, one of whom later became SEC Chairman. 1979 (C) was when the FTC charged the American Medical Association (AMA) with anti-competitive practices by unlawfully limiting consumer information access on medical service availability and prices, restricting employment on the salary of doctors by hospitals and other facilities, and banning advertising. (The FTC's orders that the AMA revoke these restrictions were then upheld by court ruling.) 1995 (D) was when the FTC established its website, www.FTC.gov.

41. A: According to research, consumers who have not formed any preconceived notions about the quality of various providers through what they have heard from others, through advertising they have seen/heard, or through their own prior experiences are more interested in price as a factor in their health care decisions. However, when consumers have traditional health insurance plans, like PPOs or HMOs (B), they are less interested in price because these plans control price. When consumers have severe or urgent medical conditions (C), they are less interested in price because

obtaining immediate care takes priority. And when they like their current health care practitioners (D), they are less interested in price because they want to see the same provider(s) regardless.

42. C: The quality of a product or service—or how useful it is, how durable, etc.—is classified as soft information, which individual consumers vary in judging. In other words, soft information is subjective. Hard information is objective because it is made up of facts. For example, the weight (A) of a product; the price (B) of a product or service; or the contents (D) of a product (e.g., the ingredients in food, cosmetic, or cleaning products) are all facts and hence are examples of hard information.

43. A: Since income tax must be paid, for financial planning purposes one should use after-tax income to determine how much is available to pay living expenses and debts. Using gross income before taxes (D) is unrealistic for paying bills as part of that money goes to paying taxes. Taxpayers either have taxes withheld from their paychecks by their employers, or pay estimated taxes in advance quarterly if self-employed, or pay their total tax for past year when filing their tax returns, etc. Living expenses and debts are NOT the same thing (B): they are two separate categories. Living expenses include mortgage or rent, utilities, food, health care, etc. Debts are accumulated amounts already owed rather than new monthly bills, like credit card debt, outstanding medical bills, loan repayment, etc. Assets listed *should* include savings (C) as these fit the definition of an asset, whether one plans to spend them or not.

44. C: It can help for other people to recommend financial goals (A), especially for young people about to be graduated from high school or college and/or starting jobs. However, though others can give advice about goals, they should not tell the individual which ones to pursue (B); this is something the individuals must decide for themselves. Financial goals can include savings, investments, and spending as well (D). If someone has a goal to buy a house, car, business, etc., these are included as financial goals, so spending can be as much a part of a person's financial goals as saving and/or investing to provide for financial security and/or freedom in the future.

45. B: By law, clothing manufacturers are required to include all of this information on the labels, tags, packaging, or printed on the inside of the fabric: a registered ID number identifying the manufacturer (A); the country where the clothing was made (C); the fiber content of the garment; and the care instructions, which are also required and not optional (D).

46. D: Nutrition Facts panels on food packaging are required by law to include the serving size, number of servings per container, calories per serving; grams of protein, carbohydrates, fats, and fiber per serving; milligrams of sodium per serving; and the percentage per serving of the Daily Value for protein, carbohydrates, fats, cholesterol, and also certain vitamins and minerals.

47. D: Calcium is among several minerals and vitamins whose amounts are represented in Nutrition Facts as a percentage of the Daily Value (based on a 2,000-calorie per day diet according to the FDA, and on a 2,500-calorie a day diet according to the USDA). Unlike vitamin and mineral supplement packages, food packages do not show calcium in number of milligrams (A). Calcium in supplements is commonly measured in milligrams, not in micrograms (B) as Vitamin D is measured, but this measurement is not shown on food labels. The amount is not shown as a percentage of a serving size (C) of the food, but as a percentage of the Daily Value (DV), i.e., the percentage of how much calcium is recommended in the daily diet. For example, given a DV of 1,000 mg of calcium, the label of an 8-ounce milk container will show its calcium content as 30% rather than as 300 mg.

48. C: The cognitive bias based on representativeness occurs when a manager makes a decision based on wrongly generalizing about something that only happened once, or about a sample that is too small to be representative of an entire group. The prior hypothesis bias (A) occurs when a manager makes decisions based on beliefs s/he has previously formed about a relationship among factors, even though these beliefs are proven wrong by the evidence. The illusion of control bias (B) occurs when a manager overestimates how much s/he is able to control what will happen. The escalating commitment bias (D) occurs when a manager has already committed significant resources to a project, and then after problems with it are revealed through feedback, commits even more resources to it in an attempt to resolve the problems.

49. B: In the devil's advocacy method, one alternative at a time is presented by the group, and one group member then critiques the alternative and/or the group's process for identifying alternatives by pointing out the drawbacks. In the dialectic inquiry method, two groups each select alternatives and each group then critiques the other group's choices. Managers listen to each group's presentation and critique of alternatives. Thus the number of alternatives presented at a time is one with devil's advocacy and two with dialectic inquiry. With both methods, alternatives are reassessed (A) after being critiqued and/or debated. With both methods, an alternative may be accepted (C). With devil's advocacy, if not accepted the alternative will be rejected or modified; with dialectic inquiry, if both alternatives are not accepted, only one may be accepted; or the two may be combined. With both methods, increasing group diversity has the same effect (D): a broader range of alternatives becomes available with more diverse members contributing.

50. B: The 80/20 Rule means that 80% of our typical work activities contribute less than 20% to the value of the work we do. Therefore, if we only complete the 20% of our tasks that are most important, we still realize the majority of the value from our work. This rule is one of the primary reasons why prioritizing is an effective tool for time management. Choices (A), (C), and (D) are NOT correct definitions of the 80/20 Rule.

51. C: The eldercare.gov site helps consumers find elder-care facilities in their local communities. Typing one's ZIP code or city and state into the designated box yields a list of local facilities or one may search by topic (e.g., Alzheimer's Disease, Caregivers, Elder Abuse Prevention, Financial Assistance, Food & Nutrition, Health Insurance, Home Repair and Modification, Transportation, Volunteerism, and others). Medicare's website (A) offers an overview of options for long-term care, a tool for comparing Medicare- and Medicaid-certified nursing homes, and more. The LeadingAge website (B) gives consumers information on what to look for when taking tours of prospective nursing homes. LeadingAge is part of the International Association of Homes and Services for the Aging (IAHSA). The website of the Assisted Living Federation of America or ALFA (D) also provides consumers with a checklist to use when visiting prospective nursing homes.

52. C: Due to the recent economic recession (c. 2007–2009), many child caregivers are now offering multiple services, like housekeeping, tutoring, etc. Parents can thus get help in more areas for their money. Also because of the recession, many caregivers are charging *lower* rates, not higher (A). Another recent trend owing to economic factors is *more* parents getting help with child care from their own parents (B). (Fewer extended families lived together in the recent past than historically, but this is changing.) Some families relocate to live with/nearer to their parents, or invite their parents to live with/closer to them. This offers dual advantages of saving money on child care, and helping grandchildren and grandparents get better acquainted. Au pairs, i.e., foreign nationals, typically cost *less* in wages because parents provide their room and board as well, but State Department regulations limit their service to one-year periods, preventing longer-term provider

continuity for young children. Hence regulations are a bigger challenge than wages with au pairs, not vice versa (D).

53. D: The government's Energy Star website is best because it lists all home appliances and equipment with Energy Star labels for meeting EPA-set energy-efficiency specifications, and includes annual electricity and water use, free of charge. The Sears website (A) is good for consumers who want to buy specifically from Sears, because they can type "Energy Star appliances" into the site's search bar and it will display all Energy Star products sold by Sears. The Energy Star.gov site is better by not restricting customers to one store for buying energy-efficient home equipment and appliances. McGraw-Hill's Sweets Network site at http://products.construction.com/ (B) is an excellent site, but only for locating construction materials and building products and equipment; it does not sell appliances. The Consumer Reports website (C) rates and recommends appliances among many other products, including whether they meet Energy Star requirements; however, while consumers can read its buying guides online, they must pay for a subscription to view the actual ratings, including Energy Star information.

54. B: Experts recommend that parents choose toys that stimulate both creativity and social interaction. They advise toys that both boys and girls can play with are better (A)—which also saves money for parents with both. Experts recommend toys that stimulate several senses rather than just one at a time (C). And they find that eye-hand coordination and problem-solving skills are equally important for toys to develop, rather than one over the other (D).

55. B: All of these accurately describe women's nutritional requirements. Women differ from men not only in numbers of calories, but also in the amounts they need of various nutrients. And even among women alone, their nutritional needs will not be the same at different times during their menstrual cycles (C), or when they are pregnant, or when they are breastfeeding (nursing) infants (D).

56. C: As a group, African-American people are genetically predisposed to certain conditions including high blood pressure and high cholesterol. With this predisposition, they can be more sensitive to dietary intake of sodium and fats, which can contribute more to developing these conditions. (Some African-Americans have high cholesterol due to genetics despite their maintaining low body weights, exercising regularly, and eating low-fat diets. But a different lifestyle could make their levels even higher; and for others, lifestyle changes help, or help more combined with medication than medication alone.) It is thus not accurate that cultural diet choices cause such conditions (A), or that African-Americans' nutritional needs are no different than others' (B). While low-income African-Americans cannot afford more nutritious foods, neither can other low-income Americans; middle-income and high-income African-Americans can afford these foods; and diet does not account for genetics, hence (D) is incorrect.

57. B: Vitamin C increases the body's absorption of non-heme iron, i.e., iron from plant sources such as beans, tomatoes, prunes, spinach, pumpkins, etc. Calcium (A), vitamin D (C), and vitamin E (D) are not known to increase the absorption of iron from vegetables, fruits, and legumes.

58. C: A 1.4-oz. (40-gram) chunk of cheddar cheese has 296 mg of calcium. A 4.2-oz. (120-gram) slice of fruit cheesecake has 94 mg of calcium. A 5.3-oz. (150-gram) serving of plain low-fat yogurt has 243 mg of calcium. A 2.6-oz. (75-gram) serving of plain vanilla ice cream has 75 mg of calcium. So the yogurt is second to the cheddar cheese, the cheesecake is third, and the ice cream is fourth.

59. B: Vitamins A, D, E, and K are fat-soluble vitamins, meaning they dissolve in lipids, i.e., fats. The body absorbs these vitamins in fat globules and stores them in the tissues. Therefore, if someone ingests excessive amounts of any of these vitamins, they can build up to harmful levels. Vitamin C (A) and the complex of B vitamins (C) are water-soluble vitamins, meaning they dissolve in water and are not stored in the tissues. Any excess amounts are excreted in urine and sweat. Water-soluble vitamins do not build up in the body, but fat-soluble vitamins do. Therefore (D) is incorrect.

60. D: The USDA recommends that in a healthy meal, at least half of the plate should be made up of fruits and vegetables. Its recommendations for proteins (A) vary by age, sex, and activity level from 2 ounces to 6 ounces daily. Most Americans eat enough protein; but the USDA advises eating a greater variety of proteins, and leaner ones. Recommendations for grains {(A), (C)} also vary with age, sex, and activity from 3 to 8 ounces daily, but the USDA advises at least half of all grains we eat should be whole grains rather than refined grains. USDA recommendations for dairy foods {(B), (C)} depend on age: 2 cups daily for ages 2–3 years, 2½ cups daily for ages 4–8 years, and 3 cups daily for ages 9 years and older.

61. B: %Daily Values (DVs) make it easier for consumers to know how much of what they need daily of certain nutrients a food supplies. For example, if a food contains 33%DV of sodium, the consumer knows that food supplies 1/3 of the sodium s/he should consume in a day. This means consumers need *not* know the actual numerical amounts of nutrients they need daily, or how much of that number a food has (A); e.g., they need not know that 2400 mg of sodium is how much to consume daily, or that a food with 800 mg of sodium has 1/3 the DV. %DVs also make it *easier* for consumers to comparison shop, not harder (C); e.g., they can pick a food lower in sodium instead of one with too much. The FDA developed DVs *not* because the RDAs were inaccurate (D), but because certain nutrients the FDA wanted to require on labels did not have RDAs established for them.

62. C: By definition, bulimia is a disorder wherein the patient binge-eats excessive amounts of food and then purges it by inducing vomiting, abusing laxatives, or both. Anorexia (B), a disorder wherein the patient starves, eating almost no food, and often also exercises excessively, *sometimes* but *not always* also includes binge-eating and purging, or just purging. Therefore, (A) and (D) are incorrect.

63. B: In type 1 diabetes, the pancreas does not produce insulin, the hormone necessary for converting sugars, starches, and other foods to energy. In type 2 diabetes, the pancreas does produce insulin, but the body does not respond properly to the hormone; this is called insulin insensitivity. Both type 1 and type 2 diabetes have both genetic and environmental factors, so (A) is incorrect. While type 1 diabetes was previously called "juvenile diabetes," it can develop in childhood or young adulthood; and though most cases of type 2 diabetes used to develop during adulthood, in recent years many children and adolescents have been diagnosed with type 2 diabetes, so (C) is incorrect. Type 1 accounts for only 5% of diabetes cases while the rest are type 2, so (D) is incorrect.

64. B: One tip from nutrition experts for healthy eating is to exercise instead of eat to relieve boredom. While eating should be interesting and enjoyable, it should be done out of hunger, not boredom. Experts do advise keeping a log or diary of what foods we eat, when we eat them, why, etc. Keeping records does *not* cause obsession or compulsion (A), it is the other way around: people with obsessive-compulsive disorder or prone to obsessive-compulsive tendencies may think obsessively and behave compulsively about anything, including keeping eating records. Keeping track of eating helps most people understand their eating habits and change them if needed. Experts advise *not* skipping meals (C), which can cause unstable blood sugar levels, fatigue, and

subsequent overeating. Experts also advise people *not* to prohibit themselves from ever eating certain foods, even those considered unhealthy (D). This encourages abnormal attitudes toward food and bingeing on either the forbidden foods or allowed ones.

65. C: One component of CBT is breaking linkages or associations between eating/food and other things when those connections contribute to overeating, emotional eating, poor food choices, etc. Some techniques for breaking linkages include not eating in certain environments; not keeping poor food choices at home; finding alternatives to eating as coping mechanisms; obtaining social support; changing eating habits; using positive reinforcement, problem-solving strategies, rehearsal, etc. Another component of CBT involves positive self-statements (A), used to replace self-defeating thoughts (e.g., "I'll never change," "This is too difficult," etc.). Evaluating readiness for change (B) is a component of CBT wherein the individual becomes aware of what s/he needs to do to attain his/her weight management goals, and then commits to doing those things. Self-monitoring (D) is a component of CBT wherein one keeps track of things like food choices, portion sizes, and factors other than hunger that trigger eating. This increases eating self-awareness and supports focusing on long-term success.

66. A: When planning the menu for a meal, one should first decide what the entrée should be, as it is the "centerpiece" of the meal. The planner should then decide upon what side dishes (B) will go well with the entrée. The décor (C) should also be chosen to complement the entrée rather than vice versa. The menu should be planned first, and then the foods needed should be bought rather than buying foods first and then designing a menu to include those foods (D).

67. B: Dining etiquette dictates that hosts and guests should pass dishes to the right, not clockwise (A) with the exception of bread, which should be passed clockwise; hence (C) is incorrect. The rule for cutting up one's food is to cut up anything larger than one's thumb at the second joint rather than being up to the individual guest (D).

68. A: Food poisoning can be caused by all of these preparation factors with certain foods. For example, cooking for the wrong lengths of time (B) and/or at the wrong temperatures (C) can cause perfringens food poisoning due to the microorganism *clostridium perfringens.* Unpasteurized milk can cause illness from the bacteria *campylobacter jejuni; salmonella; E. coli* O157:H7 infection; and/or *listeria monocytogenes;* and unrefrigerated (or improperly refrigerated) meats, cream pastries, and egg or potato salads with mayonnaise can cause food poisoning from the bacterium *Staphylococcus aureus.*

69. A: Microwave ovens are by far more energy-efficient than the others named, in both cooking efficiency and energy factor. (Cooking efficiency equals the fraction of the total energy the oven consumes that is used to cook food. Energy factor equals the ratio of energy used for cooking food to the total energy consumed.) Convection ovens (B) powered by electricity are more energy-efficient than convection ovens powered by gas; and both kinds of convection ovens are more energy-efficient than traditional electric or gas ovens; but a microwave oven is about 7–8 times more energy-efficient than electric or gas convection ovens, about 5 times more efficient than standard electric ovens, and about 9–10 times more efficient than regular gas ovens. (Note that efficiency refers to energy used, not cost in money, which depends on local rates charged for electricity and gas.)

70. A: Partially hydrogenated vegetable oil is produced through a chemical reaction of liquid vegetable oil with hydrogen to make it semi-solid, as in shortening. This process creates trans fats, which contribute to heart disease. The U.S. FDA has found trans fats even more dangerous than

saturated fats. These fats raise LDL (low-density lipoproteins) or "bad" cholesterol, which clogs arteries, and lower HDL (high-density lipoproteins) or "good" cholesterol, which helps remove "bad" cholesterol from the arteries. They also promote inflammation. Fully hydrogenated vegetable oil (B) does not contain trans fat and seems harmless, as its saturated fat is converted to monounsaturated fat by the body. Monounsaturated fats (C), like olive oil, canola oil, peanut oil and peanut butter, sunflower oil, sesame oil, avocados, and many other seeds and nuts, lower LDL, can raise HDL when replacing saturated fats, decrease inflammation, and supply antioxidants that combat diseases. Polyunsaturated fats (D) like regular, nonhydrogenated vegetable oils, lower total cholesterol and LDL, and can raise HDL when replacing saturated fats.

71. A: Freeze-dried cheese is a good way to have cheese in long-term storage for emergencies, etc. However, it does cost more than fresh cheese does. Hence (B) is incorrect. Food storage experts do not recommend using freeze-dried cheese regularly to replace fresh cheeses (C). Rather, to ensure one's comfort with using it, they recommend trying it in a few of one's favorite recipes. There are two ways to reconstitute freeze-dried cheese. The quicker method—placing it on paper towels, spraying with water, stirring, and waiting—is fine for melting the cheese and using it in recipes. The method that takes longer—drizzling cold water over it in a bowl while stirring continuously, and then refrigerating in a zip-lock bag for several hours to overnight before use—rehydrates the cheese to be just like fresh cheese; hence (D) is incorrect.

72. C: Wardrobe experts advise women to use "tough love" on their closets and get rid of anything they have not worn for more than a year (A), anything that does not fit them (B), and anything that is not consistent with their personal styles (D) rather than only one of these. For women who can afford it, experts recommend that if they cannot bear to part with many such items and/or have trouble deciding which things to get rid of, to employ a personal stylist for help.

73. D: Everybody has a certain group or family of colors that are most flattering to them based on their skin tones. Experts advise getting rid of clothes with colors outside of this group as we do not look as well in them (A). They also advise keeping and buying clothes whose colors all coordinate, which makes it easiest to mix and match items into different outfits and gives the largest potential numbers of outfits we can create (C). Keeping items in less flattering colors just to provide more variety or a change of pace (C) is not the best advice, because we do not look as well wearing colors we may like to see but which don't flatter us. Others respond less favorably to us when we wear unflattering colors, and we are likely not to feel as good about how we look when we wear them.

74. A: Many color analysts use the four seasons to identify the main categories of color palettes. In this system, "Autumn" represents warm, yellow-based earth tones; "Winter" represents cool, blue-based colors and black and white; "Spring" represents bright, vibrant, clear colors; and "Summer" represents soft, light pastel tints of colors. Some color analysts use adjectives descriptive of temperaments for the same groups. In this system, "Passionate" equals "Autumn"; "Dramatic" equals "Winter"; "Vibrant" equals "Spring"; and "Romantic" equals "Summer."

75. D: An A-line skirt is widest at the hem, balancing out full hips without excess fabric to make the figure look bigger. The full profile of a circle skirt (A) can make the hips look even bigger and accentuate the thinness of thin legs below the hem. A pencil skirt (B) has a narrower hem and fits closely overall; this would exaggerate the contrast between full hips and thin legs. A fishtail skirt (C) is very narrow around the knees and then flares out below the knees. While this would disguise skinny legs, it would also magnify large hips.

76. C: Woven fabrics can be made using a plain weave, a twill weave, a satin weave, or a triaxial weave. In the plain weave, one yarn alternates going over and under the other. The two yarns at right angles are called the warp (A) and the weft (B). In the twill weave, the weft goes under and over two or more warp yarns at regular intervals. In the satin weave, each yarn goes over four or more others before crossing under another one. The low twist and long "float," or distance yarn goes between crossings, make satin smooth and shiny. In the triaxial weave, yarns go in three directions instead of only two. In addition to a warp and weft, the third yarn direction is called the whug (C). Woof (D) is not a weaving term. (In audio electronics, e.g., speakers and amplifiers, tweeters transmit high sound frequencies and woofers transmit low frequencies.)

77. B: Unfinished knitted or woven fabrics are first cleaned to remove dirt and oils from the manufacturing process. Then many fabrics are singed with heat to eliminate protruding ends of fibers, which prevents fabric pilling and promotes even color when dyeing. After singeing, cotton and other natural fibers are bleached to get rid of impurities in their natural color and appearance. Fabrics that do not respond well to bleach are treated with optical brighteners instead. Manufacturers may then Mercerize certain linens, cottons, and rayons using alkali to make them stronger, softer, more lustrous, and more readily accepting of dyes. Fabrics are then dyed to add colors.

78. D: The fabric care symbol of a square with an arc resembling a slightly slack clothesline hanging from between the top corners indicates the garment should be line-dried or hang-dried. The symbol of a square with diagonal lines in the upper left corner (A) indicates the garment should be dried in the shade (i.e., not in direct sunlight if this would fade the dye). A square with one horizontal line inside (B) indicates the garment should be dried flat. A square with three vertical lines inside (C) indicates the garment should be drip-dried.

79. C: When people buy houses with mortgages, they usually make a down payment in some amount; however, this is not always required (A). Buyers usually pay closing costs as well, but also not always (B). There are some loan programs that allow the borrower to purchase a house with no money down; and in buyers' markets (i.e., when the housing market affords the buyer more leverage), realtors can help buyers negotiate deals wherein the owner or seller pays some or all of the closing costs. While some buyers want to eliminate a down payment, many others prefer to pay something down to lower their subsequent monthly mortgage payment: paying nothing down results in higher monthly payments (D).

80. A: In the real estate business, it is most common for some realtors to represent buyers and others to represent sellers. Realtors typically do not represent both {(B), (C)}. This does not typically vary by the individual realtor (D), as realtors usually represent either home buyers or home sellers.

81. B: Realtors usually advise consumers to obtain pre-approval before they decide to bid on a particular house for several reasons. For example, through the pre-approval process, consumers can meet in person or online with different lenders and learn about various loan options; this helps them discover how much money they can afford to spend (A) and which loan programs will meet their needs best (C). Another reason that realtors suggest obtaining pre-approval is because purchase forms for real estate commonly stipulate that the buyer applies for financing within 7 to 10 days or some other limited period of time. It can be difficult to locate a lender and undergo a credit check that quickly, and the time pressure can cause consumers to make poor financing decisions. However, if they have found loan officers and loan programs ahead of time, it is much easier to make a well-informed decision and complete a financing application within the time limit.

82. C: One might assume that the term "first-time buyer" refers to anybody who has never owned any real property before (A), but this is not true in the realty market. In most U.S. states, this term actually refers to anyone who has not owned property within the past three years. It does not refer to anyone who has owned real estate property for less than six months (B), or to anyone who once owned but does not currently own any real estate property (D).

83. A: Today, consumers can apply for mortgage loans from diverse sources including mortgage bankers and mortgage brokers, but these are not the only sources (B); they can also apply at savings and loan associations, credit unions, commercial banks, mutual savings banks, and insurance companies (C); and today, more and more realtors are also able to arrange mortgage financing for home buyers (D).

84. C: Home buyers need to get home warranty and insurance coverage at the closing of the sale. Thus they should consult an insurance broker or a realtor before the closing to get information and make choices. It is too late to obtain insurance after the closing (A), but too early when making a bid on a house (B) since the home buyer does not know yet if s/he will end up buying the house when bidding. It would also be premature to obtain insurance when applying for a mortgage (D), which the buyer should do before making an offer for a specific house to the seller.

85. D: The UN issued its Universal Declaration of Human Rights, which includes the right to adequate housing, in 1948. The UN appointed its first Special Rapporteur on Adequate Housing (A) in 2000. The UN held its first Conference on Human Settlements, which it called Habitat I (B), in 1976. (Its second Conference on Human Settlements, called Habitat II, was held in 1996.) The UN declared the International Year of Shelter for the Homeless (C) in 1987.

86. B: One design principle embraced by some home design companies is that there should be at least three ways to get to a room in the house. They find this especially important for getting to the kitchen, which is the center of many family homes; therefore (A) is incorrect. Floor plans can be designed wherein people get to different rooms by passing through other rooms in an open floor plan, yet without disrupting how the rooms are used (C). These open floor plans make the rooms look bigger than if they were separated by halls (D) used as passageways. They also make it easier to see farther through the house.

87. D: Windows in a home can form connections to the natural environment outdoors, which also improve home experiences indoors. In addition to beautiful views when they are in the right places, windows also yield practical benefits (A) by letting in natural sunlight and fresh air. By letting in light and allowing people to see out, windows create the perception that rooms and houses look bigger, not smaller (B). However, architectural designers also need to consider factors like whether a window opens on an unattractive view, interferes with homeowners' privacy, faces in a direction that does/does not let in light at the wrong time(s) of day, etc. Therefore they must know how many windows to include and where to place them most appropriately (C) to achieve the best effects.

88. A: Concerns over climate change and protecting our environment has prompted many construction companies to research building science principles to make new houses more energy-efficient. These houses are not built in traditional ways but simply containing energy-saving appliances (B); rather, they reduce the use of energy in the house greatly from the use in a house built, for example, seven years ago. These new houses are built not only to minimize the carbon footprint, i.e., the environmental impact, of those living in them; they are also built to cost

homeowners less in energy expenses and to make living there more comfortable for them (C). Building scientists find that heating and cooling are what consume the most energy in houses, not electronics (D).

89. C: The Betty Lamp is not a modern lighting innovation (A). Rather, it was a lamp widely used during colonial times in early America, which gave a relatively good quality of light for the time. Because this lamp was historically used to light not only family life, but also all household industries, and because it could represent the enlightenment that the American Association of Family and Consumer Sciences (AAFCS) is dedicated to providing, the AAFCS adopted it as its official symbol (D) in 1926.

90. D: The AAFCS states that its leadership works not only to enhance the well-being of individuals, families, and communities (A), but also to influence how consumer goods and services are developed, delivered, and evaluated (B), and to influence both general social change and specific public policymaking (C).

91. B: None of these organizations is a part of the AAFCS. All three of them are parts of the Association for Career and Technical Education (ACTE), the biggest national education association in America dedicated to preparing young and adult people for career success through advancing education. However, the AAFCS and ACTE are related in that the ACTE has a division devoted to family and consumer sciences, of which (A), (C), and (D) are all sections.

92. D: As researchers point out and history confirms, individual women (B) such as Susan B. Anthony, Elizabeth Cady Stanton, and others, and the women's movements (C) they started have been more instrumental in fighting for and winning women's rights than state institutions (A) have been. In a similar vein, some researchers propose that national policy and law must be more proactive to undo gender stereotypes.

93. A: The Morrill Act funded land grants to U.S. states to create agricultural colleges. This law did enable these colleges to educate farmers in agricultural techniques (B); however, the way it furthered domestic sciences in America specifically was by enabling these same colleges to educate the farmers' wives in household management (A). The Turner Plan, written by Illinois College's Professor Jonathan Baldwin Turner, gave states equal land grants for agricultural colleges. However, the Morrill Act, also written by Turner and introduced by Vermont congressman Justin Smith Morrill, did *not* allocate *equal* land grants to all states (C), but grants of variable sizes according to how many congressional representatives and senators each state had. This favored the eastern states, which had larger populations. The Morrill *Anti-Bigamy* Act, also passed in 1862 by President Abraham Lincoln, banned bigamy and limited church/nonprofit land ownership (D), targeting the Utah Territory's Mormons; however, its enforcement was *not* funded; Lincoln never enforced it; and it did not further domestic sciences.

94. B: The United Nations has UN Women, the UN Entity for Gender Equality and the Empowerment of Women. UN Women has held panel discussions, such as in Geneva (2011) on countering negative gender stereotypes and discrimination as part of its Economic and Social Council (ECOSOC)'s session. The UN also includes the Commission on the Status of Women (CSW). It states the UN General Assembly (UNGA), CSW, and ECOSOC "have been addressing this issue over time and need to continue to keep a vigil, and strengthen norms to change the cosmography of gender stereotyping." The UN's 2011n panel aimed not only to examine gender stereotyping's impact, but also to combat it and to identify "effective policies and norms." Therefore (D) is incorrect. The UN's advisory and technical services not only further role models and best practices, but also

"implement, monitor and evaluate programmes," and these services are in addition to "advocacy, knowledge brokering, strategic partnerships including with CSOs, media and private sector." Thus (C) is incorrect.

95. D: Of the choices given, the most appropriate question to ask in a job interview would be when the employer would want the applicant to begin work if hired because it relates directly to the job and reflects a realistic consideration. Asking about changing his or her schedule if hired (A) could reflect a less than responsible attitude, which could negatively influence the interviewer. Asking what kind of work the employer does (B) would betray the applicant's lack of preparation and information about the company, which s/he should have researched before the interview. Asking whether s/he is hired (C) during the interview, even at its end, would be premature because hiring decisions are often made only after all applicants have been interviewed, or at the least after that applicant's interview rather than during it, and would moreover place the interviewer in an awkward position.

96. D: Problem-solving skills are among the critical thinking skills needed not only for academic activities, but also in real life including household management. Consumer and family sciences teach these. The first thing necessary to solve a problem is to identify what the problem is. Identifying different actions that could be taken (A); predicting what the results of those actions might be (B); and collecting information related to the problem (C) depend on, and cannot be done without, first defining the specific problem to be solved.

97. C: The competency quoted is Competency 4.2.2 under Content Standard 4.2, "Analyze developmentally appropriate practices to plan for early childhood, education, and services" under National Standard 4.0, Education and Early Childhood, whose comprehensive standard is, "Integrate knowledge, skills, and practices required for careers in early childhood, education, and services." The standard for Family (A) is National Standard 6.0, whose comprehensive standard is, "Evaluate the significance of family and its effects on the well-being of individuals and society." Human Development (B) is National Standard 12.0, whose comprehensive standard is "Analyze factors that influence human growth & development." Family and Community Services (D) is National Standard 7.0, whose comprehensive standard is "Synthesize knowledge, skills, and practices required for careers in family & community services."

98. A: "Demonstrate safe and environmentally responsible waste disposal and recycling methods" is Competency 8.2.10 under Content Standard 8.2, "Demonstrate food safety and sanitation procedures". "Demonstrate professional skills in safe handling of knives, tools, and equipment" (B) is Competency 8.5.1 of Content Standard 8.5, "Demonstrate professional food preparation methods and techniques for all menu categories to produce a variety of food products that meet customer needs." "Demonstrate procedures for safe and secure storage of equipment and foods" (C) is Competency 8.3.5 of Content Standard 8.3, "Demonstrate industry standards in selecting, using, and maintaining food production and food service equipment." "Use computer based menu systems to develop and modify menus"   (D) is Competency 8.4.1 of Content Standard 8.4, "Demonstrate menu planning principles and techniques based on standardized recipes to meet customer needs."

99. D: "Demonstrate procedures for assuring guest or customer safety" is Competency 10.4.6 of Content Standard 10.4, "Demonstrate practices and skills involved in lodging operations." "Apply industry standards for service methods that meet expectations of guests or customers" (A) is Competency 10.3.1 of Content Standard 10.3, "Apply concepts of quality service to assure customer satisfaction." "Examine lodging, tourism, and recreation customs of various regions and countries" (B) is Competency 10.5.1 of Content Standard 10.5, "Demonstrate practices and skills for travel

- 78 -

related services." "Apply facility management, maintenance, and service skills to lodging operations" (C) is Competency 10.4.6 of Content Standard 10.4, "Demonstrate practices and skills involved in lodging occupations."

100. C: "Analyze physical, emotional, social, spiritual, and intellectual development" is Competency 12.1.1 of Content Standard 12.1. "Analyze the effect of heredity and environment on human growth and development" (A) is Competency 12.2.1 under Content Standard 12.2: "Analyze conditions that influence human growth and development." "Analyze the effects of gender, ethnicity, and culture on individual development" (B) is Competency 12.2.3, also under Content Standard 12.2 (above). D. "Analyze the role of communication on human growth and development" (D) is Competency 12.3.2 under Content Standard 12.3: "Analyze strategies that promote growth and development across the life span."

101. C: This competency is Competency 14.1.1 of Content Standard 14.1, "Analyze factors that influence nutrition and wellness practices across the life span." An example of one competency under Content Standard 14.2, "Evaluate the nutritional needs of individuals and families in relation to health and wellness across the life span" (A) is Competency 14.2.1: "Analyze the effect of nutrients on health, appearance, and peak performance." Under Content Standard 14.5, "Evaluate the influence of science and technology on food composition, safety, and other issues" (B), an example of one competency is Competency 14.5.1: "Analyze how scientific and technical advances influence the nutrient content, availability, and safety of foods." Under Content Standard 14.4, "Evaluate factors that affect food safety from production through consumption" (D), an example of one competency is Competency 14.4.1: "Analyze conditions and practices that promote safe food handling."

102. B: The competency quoted is Competency 16.3.1 under Content Standard 16.3, "Demonstrate fashion, apparel, and textile design skills." Under Content Standard 16.2, "Evaluate fiber and textile products and materials" (A), an example of one competency is Competency 16.2.2: "Evaluate performance characteristics of textile fiber and fabrics." Under Content Standard 16.4, "Demonstrate skills needed to produce, alter, or repair fashion, apparel, and textile products" (C), an example of one competency is Competency 16.4.5: "Demonstrate basic skills for producing and altering textile products and apparel." Under Content Standard 16.7, "Demonstrate general operational procedures required for business profitability and career success" (D), an example of one competency is Competency 16.7.1: "Analyze legislation, regulations, and public policy affecting the textiles, apparel, and fashion industries."

103. C: One disadvantage of instruction using the laboratory method is that lab experiments and other procedures consume more time than other learning methods, and the apparatus used in labs can be very expensive. The experiential nature of the lab method means that students learn by actually doing things instead of by reading about or being told about them, which is an advantage (A). Students generally learn better when they receive material through multiple sensory modalities; this is another advantage of the lab method (B). An additional advantage of the lab method is that through hands-on experience and discovery, it prepares students directly for many processes they will encounter in real life (D).

104. C: One advantage of the demonstration method of instruction is that watching the instructor actually perform a process, conduct an experiment, etc., both stimulates their curiosity to learn how things are done and also sharpens their skills of observation. Other advantages include that it is systematic; it wastes less in resources, effort, and time than when students experiment themselves; and it avoids the trial and error process students often undergo when doing it themselves.

Disadvantages of this method include that students can become more passive by being observers than when they actively engage in hands-on learning, and can become more dependent on the teacher to show them things (A); demonstrations work best with small classes (B), but many classes are so large they make demonstrations ineffective; though students learn from demonstrations, the teacher's instructions and actual demonstration are very time-consuming (D); and the teacher must have sufficient expertise for an effective demonstration.

105. B: Research into business communication has demonstrated that poor communication in an organization eventually causes individual employees to mistrust each other. This research also shows that poor communication undermines quality (A); compromises productivity (C); and causes not only lack of understanding among members, but also development of anger (D) among individuals in an organization. Researchers conclude that the difference between profit and loss, or between success and failure, in a business is most often attributable to whether communication in the business is effective or not. These findings are the reasons that experts identify effective communication as the most important element of total quality management in business.

106. C: Some business experts say that five types of thinking processes are needed for strategic leadership: Critical thinking, implementation thinking, conceptual thinking, innovative thinking, and intuitive thinking. The description given defines conceptual thinking. Intuitive thinking (A) involves being able to perceive or sense some truth without any external supporting evidence or information, and to apply this perception appropriately as a factor in making the ultimate decision. Innovative thinking (B) involves being able to generate new approaches and/or ideas that produce useful opportunities and possibilities. Implementation thinking (D) involves being able to structure plans and ideas such that they can and will be carried out effectively.

107. B: Being able to analyze multiple features objectively, evaluate several different plans based on that analysis, and make a decision informed by the evaluation is an example of critical thinking, which is one of the areas whereby the FCCLA helps its members develop life skills. This example does not reflect the area of career preparation (A) because it does not involve learning job skills, identifying career interests, or making career choices. It does not reflect practical knowledge (C) as much as such examples as knowing how to stay within a budget, drive a car, do laundry, cook a meal, etc. It does not reflect interpersonal communication (D) as the student's process of analysis, evaluation, and decision-making did not necessarily involve communicating with other persons.

108. D: All of these choices reflect ways that young people can gain information on the career options available to them. Among them, the choice most likely to help them specifically identify their career interests, preferences, and goals is to participate in career assessments and in job-based exploration activities like visiting actual job sites and job shadowing (following specific employees and/or positions to learn what they do in their jobs). Career assessments help reveal the areas where students have the most aptitude and interest; and work-based exploration activities help students gain firsthand experience to identify which kinds of work they find most appealing.

109. A: FCS educators can be valuable resources for Special Education teachers by offering them consultation, team-teaching with them, and offering them strategies for teaching life skills to students with special needs. FCS educators typically are aware of alternative assessments (B) and differentiated instruction (C). Rather than their requiring Special Education teachers for team-teaching special-needs students (D), FSC educators can more often meet the needs of Special Education teachers for instructing special-needs students in Family and Consumer Sciences education by team-teaching with them.

110. C: The AAFCS' Healthy Weight Resolution was issued in 2011 to support national nutrition education and obesity prevention. The AAFCS made a resolution that a class in Life and Career Choices should be required in middle schools and junior high schools (A) in 2007. The AAFCS issued a resolution supporting education and policies that promoting health literacy (B) in 2010. The AAFCS resolved in 2003 that the 10th anniversary of the United Nations International Year of the Family should be observed (D) in 2004.

111. D: Four expectations the NATEFCS work groups identified for beginning or pre-service FCS teachers were that they *should* be able to interpret standards, criteria, and processes for evaluating FCS programs and student learning (A); that they should collect data about program effectiveness and student learning outcomes using *varied* assessments, *including* performance assessments and authentic assessments, not only normed, standardized assessments (B); that they should not only engage in personal reflection and refer to evidence from various external sources, but moreover *should* adjust their teaching practices based on this information (C); and that they should use data-based evidence to justify their decisions about program design and teaching practices (D).

112. C: Currently, food manufacturers have positions they need to fill in product development, marketing (A), consumer affairs, public policy, research (B), and strategic planning (D). Graduates of FCS programs will be most qualified to fill these positions, so food manufacturing companies hope these graduates will apply for jobs in their industry.

113. B: Today's FCS graduates who specialize in fashion and interior design must have a combination of technical knowledge, creative abilities {(A), (D)}, global awareness, and business expertise (C) for working on design teams or operating, managing, and/or owning private design businesses. No one of these is more important than the others.

114. C: Students majoring in FCS who want to become teachers will need to take additional courses in education and also do practice teaching in order to obtain a teaching certificate. The minimum degrees required for employment in the FCS field are the associate's degree or the bachelor's degree, not the master's (A). FCS students are expected to participate in internship programs in *both* four-year and two-year curriculum programs (B). FCS students will need to pursue graduate education for careers in not only teaching college, doing research, and supervising, but *also* in food and nutrition, and in teaching at extensions and in other extension jobs (D).

115. D: Students should learn never to lie on job applications; however, experts do advise that regarding experiences or events that could cast applicants in an unfavorable light, they should be as brief as possible. If employers are interested in the candidate, they will schedule an interview, wherein they can ask for more details. Students learning how to fill out job applications should also learn to fill in all requested information on the forms even if it is already on the résumé they will attach, rather than leaving it off the application (A). Students should learn to research the companies where they are applying; and it can help to tailor their application responses to emphasize the education and experience that fit a certain job best (B). Neat handwriting, correct spelling, and following directions on application forms *do* matter, and in themselves make as favorable an impression as sloppy writing, misspelling, and not following directions make an unfavorable one (C).

116. A: One good piece of advice for job applicants preparing for interviews is, when answering questions about themselves, they should support statements they make about their own positive attributes with specific examples to illustrate those qualities whenever they can. However, it is not good advice to avoid eye contact with interviewers (B). This would be good advice in Japan, where

direct eye contact is found intimidating and is avoided; but in America, it is a sign that one is paying attention and is interested in the conversation. Avoiding eye contact in job interviews in America can be interpreted as a lack of confidence or as dishonesty. Applicants should be prepared not only to answer questions, but also to ask them (C). Applicants can ask interviewers what the company is looking for in an employee; interviewers' responses can provide applicants with opportunities to explain how they meet those needs. If applicants do not understand an interviewer question, they should not try to hide it (D), but rather should request clarification.

117. A: In résumés, those with work experience should place their job histories first; students with no work history should place their educational histories first. When writing one's educational or work history in a résumé, one should list the most recent item first and work backward, not vice versa (B). One should NOT include personal references in the résumé itself (C). For employers who request personal references, the applicant should submit these separately. Résumés should NOT include reasons for leaving previous jobs (D). If these are relevant, they can be addressed during job interviews.

118. C: The principle of not exploiting people is under the Conflict of Interest category of the AAFCS Principles of Professional Practice in its Code of Ethics. The Professional Competence (A) category includes principles related to credentials; professional development; education, training, experience; claims of competence; and practice within legal limits. The Respect for Diversity (B) category pertains to practices that support diversity and respecting differences in cultural beliefs and backgrounds. The Confidentiality (D) category covers trust, respect, cooperation and confidentiality, and protecting people's confidential information in professional relationships.

119. B: Making ethically sound decisions is a principle under the Integrity heading of the AAFCS Code of Ethics Principles of Conduct. Protecting private information (A) is a principle under the Confidentiality heading of these principles. Practicing within the limits of one's expertise (C) is a principle under the Professional Competence heading. Treating consumers, as well as colleagues, individuals, and families, with fairness (D) and avoiding divided loyalties is a principle under the Conflict of Interest heading.

120. B: In the AAFCS Code of Ethics, in its Statement of Principles of Professional Practice, the category of Professional Competence includes the principle that "AAFCS members claim competence in area(s) for which they have education, training, and experience." The only concept that overlaps across the principles of Integrity and Confidentiality (D) and Conflict of Interest (A) is that of avoiding exploitation. Respect for Diversity (C) does not involve claims of competence, but rather having respect for and supporting differences among people's beliefs, backgrounds, and cultures.